James Joyce's
DUBLINERS

James Joyce's
DUBLINERS

Critical Essays
edited by
CLIVE HART

THE VIKING PRESS
NEW YORK

Published in 1969 by The Viking Press, Inc.
625 Madison Avenue, New York, N.Y. 10022

Library of Congress catalog card number: 69–18004

Printed in Great Britain

Of the fifteen essays, all originally written for this volume, "Counter-parts" by Robert Scholes and "Two Gallants" by A. Walton Litz appear also in the Viking Critical Library edition of *Dubliners*, edited by Scholes and Litz. None of the others are published elsewhere.

CONTENTS

7

PREFACE

Dubliners was first published in 1914, after Joyce had finally won his ten-year battle to let the Irish people, as he put it, take 'one good look at themselves in my nicely polished looking-glass'. The story of that struggle, of the book's genesis, and of the numerous additions which were made to the text as a result of the delays is too well known to need repetition here. (The details may be found in Ellmann's biography, and in the recently issued second volume of the *Letters*.)

It is only in recent years, however, that *Dubliners*, although frequently discussed in general terms, has begun to receive the detailed critical attention which it plainly deserves. This book attempts to carry the critical scrutiny a stage further by presenting a set of fifteen essays, one to each story, and each by a different hand. All of the essays, which are here published for the first time, were written independently by established Joyce scholars and critics. In planning the book I attempted to impose no uniformity of approach, preferring to encourage the diversity of method of, for example, Professor Hayman's carefully restrained reading of 'A Mother', Professor Kain's wide-ranging thoughts on 'Grace', Mr Halper's juxtapositions of key points from 'The Boarding House', and Mrs Glasheen's accurate adoption of Joyce's own imitative style in her essay on 'Clay'. I hope that the varied critical assumptions of the writers will serve to emphasize and illuminate the richness of Joyce's work.

The supplementary notes which appear in the Appendix are not intended to provide a comprehensive commentary, but have been supplied by the critics concerned in conformity with the particular emphases which they have chosen to adopt.

Conventions and Abbreviations

The ten-year wait for first publication seemed, to Joyce, inordinately long, but it is brief in comparison with the subsequent period of fifty-three years which elapsed before the appearance of the first scholarly edition. Robert Scholes' text (London, Jonathan Cape, 1967, and New York, Viking Press, Inc., 1968) now supersedes all others. Quotations and page-references in this work have been made to conform to his text. Page-references have been included in parentheses after substantial quotations from *Dubliners*, but in view of the brevity of most of the stories I have not thought it necessary to include such references after short illustrative quotations.

Quotations from Joyce's other works are based on the following editions:

Stephen Hero, London, Jonathan Cape, 1960, and New York, New Directions, 1955.

A Portrait of the Artist as a Young Man, London, Jonathan Cape, 1968, and New York, The Viking Press, Inc. (Compass paperback), 1964.

Ulysses, London, The Bodley Head, 1960, and New York, Random House, 1961.

Finnegans Wake, London, Faber and Faber, 1939, and New York, The Viking Press, Inc., 1939.

Where the pagination differs, the first figure corresponds to the British edition, the second to the American.

The following abbreviations are used in footnotes:

Ellmann: R. Ellmann, *James Joyce*, London and New York, 1959.

Letters I, II, III: *Letters of James Joyce*, vol. I, London and New York, 1957; vols. II and III, London and New York, 1966.

Acknowledgements

The following presses have kindly granted permission to quote from Joyce's works: Jonathan Cape Ltd and the Viking Press, Inc., for quotations from *Dubliners*; Jonathan Cape Ltd and New Directions Publishing Corp., for quotations from *Stephen Hero*; Jonathan

Cape Ltd and The Viking Press, Inc., for quotations from *A Portrait of the Artist as a Young Man*; The Bodley Head Ltd and Random House Inc., for quotations from *Ulysses*; Faber and Faber Ltd and The Viking Press Inc., for quotations from *Letters of James Joyce*.

We are also grateful to the following presses for permission to quote from critical and other works: Oxford University Press, New York, for a passage from Robert M. Adams, *Surface and Symbol*; Faber and Faber Ltd and The Viking Press, Inc., for a passage from Joseph Campbell and Henry Morton Robinson, *A Skeleton Key to Finnegans Wake*; University of Oklahoma Press for a passage from William Powell Jones, *James Joyce and the Common Reader*; Faber and Faber Ltd and Cornell University Press for a passage from Stanislaus Joyce, *The Dublin Diary of Stanislaus Joyce*; Faber and Faber Ltd and The Viking Press Inc., for a passage from Stanislaus Joyce, *My Brother's Keeper*; Chatto & Windus Ltd and Indiana University Press for passages from Hugh Kenner, *Dublin's Joyce*; John Murray Publishers Ltd for a passage from Shane Leslie, *Long Shadows*; Faber and Faber Ltd and New Directions Publishing Corp., for passages from Harry Levin, *James Joyce: A Critical Introduction*; New York University Press for a passage from Marvin Magalaner and Richard M. Kain, *Joyce: The Man, the Work, the Reputation*; Oxford University Press and Yale University Press for passages from W. M. Schutte, *Joyce and Shakespeare*; Indiana University Press for a passage from *James Joyce Today*; Columbia University Press for a passage from Kevin Sullivan, *Joyce Among the Jesuits*; Thames & Hudson International Ltd and Farrar, Straus & Giroux, Inc. (Noonday Press), for a passage from William York Tindall, *A Reader's Guide to James Joyce*; University of Chicago Press for passages from Richard M. Weaver, *Ideas Have Consequences*; Macmillan & Co. Ltd, Crowell, Collier & Macmillan, and Mr Michael Butler Yeats for lines from W. B. Yeats, 'Sailing to Byzantium'.

Our thanks are also due to the administrators of the James Joyce Estate for permission to quote from his works, and to Helen Hart and Joan Budgen, for their many hours of painstaking editorial assistance.

CLIVE HART

The Sisters

John William Corrington

I

Of all the clearly identifiable themes set forth in *Dubliners*, none is so universal or basic to the book's total meaning as are the closely linked themes of corruption, frustration, and the dream of escape. There is no story in the collection in which these themes are not operative and of central importance. It must be understood that the themes are presented in various ways – sometimes obviously, sometimes covertly. In certain stories the themes are almost subterranean in their operations, while in others the straightforwardness of their presentation nearly amounts to an artistic liability.

There is no need, I think, to attempt a definition of corruption or frustration in connection with *Dubliners*. However, it may be helpful to set forth briefly what constitutes the dream of escape. The basic idea is suggested by a long essay of Richard Weaver's wherein he discusses the 'metaphysical dream,' common to us all,[1] which

'... is an intuitive feeling about the immanent nature of reality, and this is the sanction to which both ideas and beliefs are ultimately referred for verification.'[2]

Paraphrased for our purposes and adapted to the context of *Dubliners*, we find that, in place of the 'metaphysical dream', among Dubliners there is, almost universally, a dream of escape. 'Without the

[1] Richard M. Weaver, *Ideas Have Consequences*, Chicago 1948, p. 18: 'Every man participating in a culture has three levels of conscious reflection: his specific ideas about things, his general beliefs or convictions, and his metaphysical dream of the world.'
[2] *Idem.*

13

metaphysical dream', Weaver says, 'it is impossible to think of men living together harmoniously over an extent of time. The dream carries with it an evaluation, which is the bond of spiritual community.'[1]

But, of course, Joyce has told us that the 'bond of spiritual community' in Dublin has parted, that the 'special odour of corruption' hangs over Ireland, and that Dublin is the centre of the paralysis which spreads throughout the country.

Family relations have degenerated as we see in 'Counterparts', 'The Boarding House', and 'A Little Cloud'. Politics is a hopeless dumb-show over which the ghost of Parnell broods as the shade of Shakespeare will haunt the library sequence in *Ulysses*. Religion is simply a net to trap the spirit of those born in Ireland who would fly. The metaphysical dream, in short, has decayed completely. As W. M. Schutte puts it:

'One of the major causes of the enervation in Dublin is the lack of any integrating force in the lives of its citizens. All of the pressures drive man away from man. There are no friends in *Ulysses*; there are only acquaintances . . . Not even in the married state is understanding and genuine companionship to be found . . .

'The forces in society which are assumed by the inhabitants to be capable of integrating Dublin life are seen in *Ulysses* to be every bit as maimed and impotent as they were in *Dubliners*. Of religion one hears much talk, but one finds no indication that it can help man to a balanced, creative life . . .

'Another potential integrating force, the political, is equally ineffective. The inconsistencies and divisions in nationalist thinking, which were treated briefly in "Ivy Day in the Committee Room", are developed at some length in the *Portrait* . . . In *Ulysses* the instability of Irish political life is kept constantly in the reader's mind . . .

'All of these factors, and others as well, combine to make the Dublin of *Ulysses* a city in which no creative relationships can exist. Man is alienated both from his fellow man and from the vigorous ideals and bold dreams on which alone a living social organism can thrive.'[2]

At the heart of Dublin there is nothing but memory, cant, misery, and self-pity. 'Nothing good can be done if the will is wrong', Richard Weaver says, echoing Dante, and his remark could serve

[1] *Idem.*

[2] W. M. Schutte, *Joyce and Shakespeare*, New Haven, 1957, pp. 139-41.

well enough as an epigraph to *Dubliners*; in the stories, there are few examples of right will. For the most part, will has broken down altogether, and in the ruins the metaphysical dream has been transformed into the dream of escape. There is no longer thought of harmony; the mediaeval synthesis is smashed, and even Catholic Ireland totters in the backwash of a renaissance which has killed as well as given birth, a reformation which has deformed as much as reformed, and an enlightenment which has left all of western civilization without values, purpose or faith. Schutte goes on to say:

'In *Dubliners* one pattern comes to the fore time after time: the protagonist of a story (whether an individual or a group) is placed in a position which reveals the direction he must take if he is to live a full and creative life; but always he is defeated by the combined forces of his environment. The opportunity to achieve a satisfactory integration of his life often seems within his grasp, but as he reaches tentatively toward it, he is thwarted by the conditions which the modern world imposes on him.'[1]

Now the community rests upon use rather than union: in many of the stories Joyce shows the venality which replaced spirituality in Dublin. The gold coin's implications in 'Two Gallants'; the metaphor of commerce chosen by Father Purdon in 'Grace'; the overriding concern for payment in 'Ivy Day'; the motif of simony in 'The Sisters' – all show Joyce's basic agreement with Weaver that the metaphysical dream, that spiritual consensus which undergirded the mediaeval European community, has been replaced by a nightmare of materialism in which 'work is use and not worship'.

'We know how to reward the carpenter *qua* carpenter; we do not know how to reward the egotist who comes with assertions of how much he is worth. That payment to labor which merely reflects the outcome of a tug of war is removed from philosophical determination,'[2] Weaver says, discussing the metaphysical dream's bankruptcy and its replacement by the senseless values of materialism. But Joyce carries the portrayal of collapse yet a little further. The nightmare of materialism, after all, is but a transient phase in the philosophical and moral collapse Joyce is sketching in *Dubliners*. His 'chapter of moral history' is not simply a record of greed or venality. Beyond greed lies fear, satiety, frustration. Even when greedy impulses are fulfilled, the fulfilment does not answer. Possession entraps

[1] *Ibid.*, p. 136. [2] Weaver, *op. cit.*, p. 75.

15

possessor as surely as non-possession entraps him who lacks. Joyce notes his concern for these trapped souls in *Stephen Hero*: '. . . there was no face that passed him on its way to its commercial prison but he strove to pierce to the motive centre of its ugliness.' (35-6, 30) Each is corrupted, and from this corruption is generated what I have called the dream of escape. It is, as we will see, a kind of perverted burlesque of the metaphysical dream in which all the elements of that harmonizing vision are reversed: in the dream of escape the realization of one's place in the order of things is lost. The dreamer yearns for higher position, for success, for money, for prestige. The dream of escape is always egocentric. One is chiefly concerned with oneself (the most obvious example of this is Mr Duffy in 'A Painful Case'). There is, of course, massive though understated irony in most of the stories, since the personality of characters brooding over escape is frequently itself instrumental in the creation and further-ance of the environment which is destroying them.

Joyce seems to have had in mind, as he composed *Dubliners*, a kind of basic duality. As Harry Levin sees it:

'When Joyce first set out to write, he defined the double responsi-bility of the imaginative writer as a task of mediation between the world of reality and the world of dreams. The dissonance between these two worlds, between the imminent realities of the present and the buried dreams of the past, made this task all but impossible.'[1]

There is illusion and reality. In each of the stories one finds, in varying forms, an explicit or implicit hope of escape from one or another kind of corruption, which hope is frustrated by some failure or inadequacy on the part of the dreamer, or by the nature of Dublin's influence on him. W. M. Schutte comments on this cycle:

'Most of the stories end in frustration for a central character . . . Sometimes the failure is recognized, or partially recognized, and the victim lashes back ineffectively at his world, as when Little Chandler shouts at his baby or when Farrington beats his child. Sometimes the failure is unrecognized by the character, at least in its full implications, as in "Clay" and "A Mother".'[2]

On the same subject, Levin says:

'In every one of these fifteen case histories, we seem to be reading in the annals of frustration – a boy is disappointed, a priest suffers

[1] Harry Levin, *James Joyce: A Critical Introduction*, London, 1944, p. 155; New York, 1941, p. 221.   [2] Schutte, *op. cit.*, p. 137.

disgrace, the elopement of "Eveline" fails to materialize. Things almost happen. The characters are arrested in mid-air.'[1]

As in Sartre's famous play, there seems to be 'no exit' from the soul-crushing rondo of dream and frustration for Dublin's citizens. In comparing Joyce's stories with those of Chekhov, Marvin Magalaner points out this continuous theme:

'All novelists, of course, deal in some way with the struggle of the individual against the world and against his inner self. But Joyce and his Russian counterpart [Chekhov] are alike in more specific ways. They are concerned with the same kinds of characters and situations. Avoiding Maupassant's overt action, they deal, as Matthew Josephson has pointed out, with "people who find themselves in a trap, or a 'box' . . . who plan to escape . . . But nothing happens, or at least nothing happens as they planned . . ." To mention Joyce's main characters is to establish a gallery of thwarted escapees: Farrington, Eveline, Gabriel, Little Chandler, the boy in "An Encounter", and Polly Mooney's husband.'[2]

The almost circular motion of the stories, in narrative as well as in theme, seems to adumbrate the shape of *Finnegans Wake*. 'The Sisters' starts in darkness with a boy staring at a window, speaking of the dead, seeing the window lighted 'faintly', feeling his 'soul receding into some pleasant and vicious region'. Similarly, at the end of the final story, 'The Dead', Gabriel Conroy stares at the window where snow falls 'faintly' in the darkness, thinking of the dead, 'his soul had approached that region where dwell the vast hosts of the dead'. Both 'The Sisters' and 'The Dead' are, in Hugh Kenner's phrase, 'dominated by two wraith-like sisters'.[3] In the first story, a priest lies dead in his coffin; in 'The Dead', guests at the Misses Morkan's party speak of an order of monks who sleep in their coffins.

Corruption and reality are synonymous in *Dubliners*; the dream of escape and its frustration underlies and lends continuity and form to the whole of *Dubliners*. Joyce's ability to vary and alter the triune themes is little short of marvellous. The statement of them begins in 'The Sisters'.

---

[1] Levin, *op. cit.*, pp. 29, 30.
[2] Marvin Magalaner and Richard M. Kain, *Joyce: The Man, the Work, the Reputation*, New York, 1956, p. 61.
[3] Hugh Kenner, *Dublin's Joyce*, London, 1955, and Bloomington, 1956, p. 63.

II

In this first story, the triple-theme has a complex kind of double-statement. At first there is the case of the young narrator through whose eyes we see the action. The boy has no parents. He endures well enough the life provided by his aunt and uncle, but there is boredom in it. He must listen to the windy clichés of his uncle:

' – That's my principle, too, said my uncle. Let him learn to box his corner. That's what I'm always saying to that Rosicrucian there: take exercise. Why, when I was a nipper every morning of my life I had a cold bath, winter and summer. And that's what stands to me now. Education is all very fine and large . . .' (8-9, 11)

The 'Persia' motif which we find developed in the boy's dream, a motif later restated in the 'Wild West' and 'sailor' elements of 'An Encounter', and in the 'Araby' element of the story by that name, is prefigured in the uncle's slighting reference to his nephew as 'that Rosicrucian there'. The implications of mysticism, detachment, the oriental and exotic – all intended by the uncle to stand in comic contrast to the small boy, in fact tend to round out or at least indicate his character and outlook.

Old Cotter, a family friend, adds to the monotony and dreariness with his tiresome and pointless babbling, his beginning sentences and not finishing them. He tells the boy's aunt and uncle it would be better were the boy not to visit Father Flynn, the old paralysed priest.

' – It's bad for children, said old Cotter, because their minds are so impressionable. When children see things like that, you know, it has an effect . . .' (9, 11)

Cotter speaks of children as 'impressionable', little realizing that the boy has already been impressed, that he has seen 'paralysis' and its deadly work in a way his adult relations have not. The boy's knowledge – or intuition – of corruption is considerably beyond the point at which Cotter's advice could be helpful.

But now Father Flynn is dead. And the effect Cotter has rambled on about is indeed started. When the boy goes to bed he sees again 'the heavy grey face of the paralytic'. According to his uncle, the old priest 'had a great wish' for the boy – obviously a reference to his entering the priesthood. But now the old man is gone, his trembling maladroit hands stilled for ever. Most significantly, he will no longer be there to provide a kind of romantic alternative to the boy's drab home life:

'He had studied in the Irish college in Rome and he had taught me to pronounce Latin properly. He had told me stories about the catacombs and about Napoleon Bonaparte, and he had explained to me the meaning of the different ceremonies of the Mass and of the different vestments worn by the priest.' (11, 13)

Still, despite all the old priest had done, the boy-narrator discovers not only that he feels little sorrow at the old man's death, but rather feels 'as if I had been freed from something by his death'. It is not difficult to suppose the 'something' from which he has been freed is the priesthood. But, while this is so, the situation is more complex than a reader may suppose. Because, while the boy fears the grave responsibilities of the priesthood (as he fears the word 'paralysis' and yet is drawn to it) and feels something akin to relief when the representative (and, it should be noted, an unsuccessful representative) of those responsibilities dies, he remains fascinated by the 'complex and mysterious' institutions of the church.

It is necessary to examine most carefully the dream of which the boy speaks early in the story, in which he sees Father Flynn's grey face. In the dark of the boy's room, the face pursues him even when he draws the blanket over his head. He tries to think of Christmas but the face still follows, murmuring, trying to confess something. Joyce's ability to fuse the apparently naturalistic and the clearly symbolic in a phrase is singularly exemplified here. If, on the level of naturalistic narration, thinking of Christmas is an attempt to substitute toys and fruit, a large dinner and excitement, for the morbid and frightening, on the symbolic level it would appear to be a substitution of birth for death, of the vision of the living Christ for that of his dead deputy. It is worth noting, in this context, that Joyce frequently ties Christmas and death together. In *A Portrait*, a dead man is the cause of dissension at the famous 'Christmas dinner' (27ff, 27ff) and the Twelfth-night party in 'The Dead' is the occasion for Michael Furey's shade to stalk Gabriel Conroy.

At this point, one must quote the young narrator:

'I felt my soul receding into some pleasant and vicious region; and there again I found it waiting for me. It began to confess to me in a murmuring voice and I wondered why it smiled continually . . .

it had died of paralysis and I felt that I too was smiling feebly as if to absolve the simoniac of his sin.' (9, 11)

This is the dream's first part, and in it the boy has taken over the priest's functions. This exchange of functions is a constant motif throughout 'The Sisters'. The uncle of the young narrator parodies the sacrament by offering Cotter 'a pick of that leg of mutton'. As his uncle offers a piece of the 'Lamb of God', so the young narrator himself would carry to Father Flynn his aunt's gift of 'a packet of High Toast', a parody on the Sacred Host. While most frequently commented upon, the sacramental function of Eliza and Nannie at the story's end is only the most obvious of several. The boy hears the old paralytic's confession and grants absolution; his smile mirrors that of the old man.

In the second portion of the dream, the boy tells us,

'I remembered that I had noticed long velvet curtains and a swinging lamp of antique fashion. I felt that I had been very far away, in some land where the customs were strange – in Persia, I thought. . . . But I could not remember the end of the dream.' (12, 13–14)

Here the boy's having taken over the priestly functions is abstracted. The curtain might hang behind an altar or at the door of a sacristy. The antique lamp swinging might be either the altar light, or, more likely, the censer, a highly decorated lamp-like vessel in which incense is burned during high mass or benediction – and more germanely at funerals where it is used to incense the coffin. The strange customs match, clearly enough, with the 'complex and mysterious' institutions of the church.

Thus the dream's division alerts us to Joyce's meaning: in the first part, the boy takes over the responsibilities from the old man, and becomes, in the dream, the new priest of Father Flynn's 'great wish'. But it is this aspect of the priesthood that does not please the boy. In the dream's second part, it is the liturgy, the ritual and mystery of the church, in marked contrast to the monotony and dullness of his daily life, that attracts and influences him. The situation is paralleled in *A Portrait*:

'He[Stephen] listened in reverent silence now to the priest's appeal [to join the Jesuit order] and through the words he heard even more distinctly a voice bidding him approach, offering him secret knowledge and secret power.' (162, 159)

But the priest is surrounded with death symbolism:

'The priest's face was in total shadow but the waning daylight from behind him touched the deeply grooved temples and the curves of the skull' (157, 154) and later the priest's face resembles 'a mirthless reflection of the sunken day'. (163, 160)

After Father Flynn's death, the boy feels freed from the church, but if he is 'freed' from it, he is nonetheless still attracted to the 'Persia' of Catholicism as, in later stories, he is drawn to the 'Araby' of romance or the 'Wild West' of untrammelled wandering. And the church, through the aegis of Father Flynn, has stood as one symbol of a life beyond and above the dreary repetitions of Dublin. As Kevin Sullivan has put it,

'Joyce thought longer and more seriously about becoming a Jesuit than is generally supposed or admitted . . . It would also seem that what has been called Joyce's "sacerdotalism" had its origin in this same adolescent experience, that the religion of art which he celebrated in his works was a substitute for the art of religion from which he turned away in his youth.'[1]

From the sentence 'Eliza sighed again and bowed her head in assent', and onward, the boy loses function in the story. He becomes no more than a reportorial voice. It is the dead priest and his 'crossed' life that come into sharp and immediate focus.

The old priest, we are told, was not up to the manifold responsibilities of the priesthood. In fact, he has failed his vocation. The degree and precise nature of the failure are not explained, but, symbolically, the dropped chalice is information enough. The sisters lay Father Flynn's failure to his scrupulosity. He was nervous, fearful of doing wrong, and the fear itself is part and parcel of his failure.

At this point it becomes necessary to explain, at least briefly, the primary symbolic content of the story in order to get at the full significance of its thematic meaning.

To begin, Marvin Magalaner's explication of 'The Sisters' seems faulty.[2] The old priest represents not God, after all, but the Irish church itself. Whatever the reasons, the Irish church had, to Joyce's mind, failed the Irish people. The Catholic faith in Ireland was a prime element in the general corruption and decay which Joyce pictures. The broken chalice symbolizes the church's failure. It

---

[1] Kevin Sullivan, *Joyce Among the Jesuits*, New York, 1958, p. 9.
[2] Magalaner and Kain, *op. cit.*, pp. 71-3.

would seem that Joyce's sole symbolic comment on God, as apart from the church, comes when, speaking of the broken chalice, Eliza points out that 'it contained nothing'. In symbolic terms, one is constrained to assume the reference is to the metaphysical root not only of Catholicism but of religion generally, and that the priest's failure is essentially a human failure since there is nothing of importance in the chalice of religion anyhow.

The sisters represent, I think, the Irish people: respectful of the church, ready always to serve:

' – . . . God knows we done all we could, as poor as we are – we wouldn't see him want anything while he was in it.' (14, 16)

To strengthen the notion of the sisters as symbolic representatives of the Irish people, one might note the similarity in age, speech and general demeanour between Eliza and the old milk-woman in the opening sequence of *Ulysses*. It is, by the way, in her office as representative of the Irish people that Eliza is disappointed at the boy's failure to take cream crackers and his slowness to sip sherry. It is not the church which is moved to emotion by apostasy, but the people. An example is contained in *A Portrait* when Stephen Dedalus is held and whipped by classmates for having championed Lord Byron as a great poet: ' . . . Byron was a heretic and immoral too' (83, 81), one of his tormentors cries.

It can be argued, if one accepts Father Flynn as the Irish church and the sisters as the Irish people, that the extent and profundity of paralysis and decay is the product, to a degree, of interaction between them. The sisters care for the old man as he slips deeper into decay: 'Whenever I'd bring in his soup to him there I'd find him with his breviary fallen to the floor, lying back in the chair and his mouth open.' (16, 16) Still, the old man has had a certain degree of ascendance over them. He plans a trip back to the portion of town in which they had all been born, and, even in death, he is their primary concern.

Where, precisely, does the boy stand in this relationship? Clearly he is a young and still malleable generation looking upon Ireland. Not only the sisters, but his aunt and uncle – and particularly old Cotter – represent the old priest-ridden, superstitious, and decadent state of Ireland's people. Father Flynn represents, as in the dream, the way and the life of complexity and mystery which is at least a measure of escape from Dublin's deadly tedium. The boy is not concerned much with the sisters, yet he cannot help noting the dilapidated condition in which these representatives of the Irish are to be found:

'I pretended to pray but I could not gather my thoughts because the old woman's mutterings distracted me. I noticed how clumsily her skirt was hooked at the back and how the heels of her cloth boots were trodden down all to one side.' (13, 14)

Kenner has made rather a point of what he calls 'the boot-heel world'.[1] This level of reality is played off against the 'vaguely dangerous' aspects of more complex, less immediate experience, such as are represented by the old priest. What Kenner has not said is that the boy is finally trapped between two kinds of paralysis, two kinds of corruption. At this point, the boy has not decided – has only begun to collect the information requisite to even a poorly informed decision – which mode of corruption repels him least (since it is, after all, not a world in which one may choose what attracts him most). Speaking later of the stories 'Eveline' through 'The Boarding House', Kenner says,

'The gentle lyric antitheses of the first pages are growing sharper, as the consciousness divided between the public fact and the private dream incarnates its conflicting elements in the two kinds of men and two kinds of women who people the epic phase. Later these people will start meeting one another and realize dimly that they are meeting themselves.'[2]

The public fact, as we see, is corruption; the private dream is of escape and the problem of 'meeting themselves' is to be expanded not in *Dubliners* but in *Ulysses*, when Stephen says, 'Every life is many days, day after day. We walk through ourselves, meeting robbers, ghosts, giants, old men, young men, wives, widows, brothers-in-love. But always meeting ourselves.' (273, 213)

While the sisters' symbolic value may be, in the framework of Joyce's whole *œuvre*, an important and meaningful one, the most important aspect of the story in terms of *Dubliners* is, of course, the relationship between Father Flynn and the boy-narrator.

As we have seen, the old man is a failure in his vocation. He has dropped chalice and breviary as he spills snuff through his paralysed fingers. Still he has provided the boy with diversion, has interested himself in the boy, has, for a time at least, broken the hold of Dublin's

---

[1] Kenner, *op. cit.*, pp. 51-3.   [2] *Ibid.*, p. 56.

dull grip on him. What has the old man gained? The use of a young life. Father Flynn has a 'great wish' for the boy, and in essence, that great wish is that the narrator dedicate himself to the same priest-hood, thus permitting the old man to relive, vicariously, his own youth.

Schutte sees a similar situation in *Stephen Hero* where Stephen's quarrels with his mother 'make clear that May Dedalus, spiritually alienated from her failure of a husband, has placed all of her emotional capital in Stephen . . . The futility and frustrations of her life were to be redeemed by Stephen's accession to the priesthood.'[1]

At this point, the nature of the old man's frustration becomes obvious. The priesthood has been his trap. He has been too 'scru-pulous'; he has not been able to cope with his responsibilities and from the knowledge of this failure he seeks escape. The boy, fleeing his own drab life, encounters the old man and is bemused by the complexity and mystery of the church. The old man attempts, as it were, to escape his own 'crossed' life, by proxy, through the boy. As Richard Ellmann puts it:

'Joyce allowed the priest's character to form itself through the testimony of different witnesses – the narrator . . . , the suspicious family friend and the uncle, and finally the two sisters . . . Each of these furnishes the reader with another hint of the priest's failure, of his sense of his own ruin, of his attempt in ambiguous little ways to transmit corruption to the susceptible boy.'[2]

In his dream, the boy changes places with the old man, smiles the same uncertain conspiratorial smile, offers the old man absolution of 'simony', for having tried to 'sell' him (the boy-narrator) a re-ligious vocation which he (Father Flynn) himself found too much to bear. In the dream, the boy and the old man fuse briefly: the smile between them, a mark of unspoken kinship in the faint duplicity of the Irish church. This priestly smile is echoed many times in *A Portrait* and *Ulysses*: in Stephen's description of Cranly, 'It was a priestlike face . . . priestlike in the lips that were long and bloodless and faintly smiling . . .' (181–2, 178); when Stephen sees a visiting Jesuit at the college, '. . . he watched this swaying form and tried to read for himself the legend of the priest's mocking smile . . .' (87, 84); and throughout Father Conmee's smiling excursion out of Dublin in *Ulysses*.

---

[1] Schutte, *op. cit.*, p. 108.　　[2] Ellmann, pp. 169–70.

The boy takes over, in his dream, the old man's role of confessor. The dark room serves as confessional, the blanket as screen, so that the boy acts out in his own bedroom a scene almost analogous to that final one described by Eliza in which Father Flynn is found laughing in his dark confessional. The boy, describing himself drifting into his dream, speaks of 'my soul receding into some pleasant and vicious region . . . ', and the old priest laughs in the 'pleasant and vicious' darkness of an empty confessional, the co-symbol, along with broken chalice and fallen breviary, of his lapsed priesthood. In this impenetrable darkness, Father Conmee's smug, knowing smile which we note in *Ulysses* turns into hysterical laughter of one beyond hope or illusion. If, finally, the old man is to elude the implications of the dark empty confessional, it must be through the boy. Death ends the relationship, and the old man does not know that his 'great wish' for the boy is to end as did his priesthood: in frustration.

I submit, then, that there is a kind of symbiotic partnership between the old priest and the boy-narrator of 'The Sisters'. As, in the beginning, the boy is diverted (though not deeply moved) by the old priest's stories and interest in him, and escapes in some measure the boredom of his life at home, so in turn, the old priest, in 'amusing' himself with teaching catechism and listening to the boy's Latin responses, attempts to recreate the broken chalice of his own priestly life. But as each dreams of escape through the other, each finds frustration in the relationship. The old priest dies; the boy feels, unaccountably, freed by his death. But if the boy is freed from the illusion of escape through the church, it is a freedom of questionable value, since it leaves him still locked within the matrix of Dublin's dreary world.

An Encounter

Fritz Senn

Like many of the other stories in *Dubliners*, but more explicitly than most, 'An Encounter' deals with escape. On this occasion the escape is more than vaguely desired: it is actually attempted, and there is even a measure of success.

But from the outset it is on a very limited scale. It can be brought off because it hardly goes beyond the boyish games, the Indian battles and sieges that are enacted in the evening. A 'day's miching' inevitably entails a return to home and school. There is never any plan to leave Dublin for good. The boys are not yet aware of the barrenness of their city, of its paralysis, as the more mature characters of *Dubliners* are, or as some of them discover in a series of revelations. Even less can the boys become conscious of paralysis as a psychological or moral deficiency. But while the protagonist in the three 'boyhood' stories does not yet formulate articulate thoughts about the true nature of his plight, he can still be prompted to act on impulse, a capacity which most of the adults seem to have lost.

The longing of the boy who tells 'An Encounter' – and who, as in 'The Sisters' and in 'Araby', remains unnamed, as though he had not yet attained a feeling of identity within the social framework – is at first a vague and general desire for the opening of 'doors of escape'. Later it is felt specifically as a wish to 'break out of the weariness of school-life' and its 'restraining influence'. The ultimate aim of the 'spirit of unruliness' is probably less narrow, but initially its manifestation is felt chiefly as a gesture of defiance against the life of discipline and tedium at school. The plan is accordingly formed. An excursion to the Pigeon House might easily take place during the oncoming holidays ('The summer holidays were near at

26

hand'), but it has to be arranged during term time if it is to be meaningful as a break away from school. It is similar in kind to the exploit of the cat which, chased by Mahony, 'escaped into a wide field'.

The spirit of unruliness which diffuses itself among the boys is never allowed much scope and must, in its turn, be canalized according to a set of established rules. The battles and the sieges have to be 'arranged', the warfare is 'mimic'. In like manner the miching has to be carefully planned, excuses have to be written – for the gesture of defiance must not be recognized as such – sixpences have to be saved up and a time scheme is to be adhered to in order to avoid detection. The whole enterprise requires a degree of conformity not markedly different from that which characterizes the daily routine.

Given all these limitations, however, it is worth noting (especially in view of most critics' heavy emphasis on paralysis) that the escape does take place. Two boys do get away from the weariness of school-life for at least one day. The feat demands a level of courage to which only two out of three boys can rise. The third, a member of a family that shows all the earmarks of conventional respectability and inertia, fails to turn up. In a city as much given over to conformity as Joyce's Dublin, to get away even for a short time from an institution which includes such disciplinarians as Father Butler and Mr Ryan is already an achievement.

But of course the success of the enterprise is severely qualified. Not only is the expedition reduced in strength, but the final destination, the Pigeon House, is never reached. As a striving *towards* something it is a failure. The doors of escape are not really passed, the boys are unable to 'walk out', the Pigeon House remains beyond their grasp. The trip ends anticlimactically on a sloping field near the river Dodder, whose very name seems to suggest weakness and unsteadiness. The story might well close here, with the silent, tired boys left to their 'jaded thoughts', ready to avail themselves of the train service as a part of that order which they had tried to leave behind.

Yet while the quest falls short of its proposed aim it is unexpectedly supplemented by an adventure that was not part of the plan – an encounter with an elderly man of strange habits and disquieting talk. The boy who reflected that 'real adventures . . . do not happen to people who remain at home' is confronted with something entirely unlike anything he might read in adventure stories, but which is very real indeed. The encounter which gives the story its title results in the detection of a reality unknown to him before.

Joyce's early prose works could be summarized as stages in the growing awareness of reality, brought about by a succession of encounters with that reality. In *A Portrait of the Artist as a Young Man*, which depicts the development of a boy and adolescent, the repeated use of thematic words is an important aspect of the technique. Under the influence of his reading the boy starts out with romantic notions about a 'holy encounter' which will contrast with 'the horrible reality which lay between his hope of then and now'. (*A Portrait*, 102, 99) At a later stage Stephen's will seemed 'drawn to go forth to encounter reality' (162, 159), the reality being different in each case and always other than was anticipated. The *Portrait* ends with the exalted and programmatic declaration: 'I go to encounter for the millionth time the reality of experience and to forge in the smithy of my soul the uncreated conscience of my race'. (257, 252-3) *Ulysses* too is a series of encounters with reality. It is obvious that Joyce's first literary expression of such an encounter is unlikely to be simple or easy to define.

As in many other works of Joyce 'An Encounter' draws on earlier literature for much of its psychological impetus. The idea of the Wild West is first 'introduced' by means of a 'little library', before it is carried over into life in the form of mock battles and plans of campaign. The written word opens doors of escape, but it can also become a means of evading confrontation with reality, a substitute for any vital impulse towards life, as in the case of the man who 'had all Sir Walter Scott's works and all Lord Lytton's works at home and never tired of reading them'. A corresponding development is hinted at in Father Butler's strictures on the presumed author of *The Apache Chief*: 'The man who wrote it, I suppose, was some wretched scribbler that writes these things for a drink.' The reading as well as the writing – sometimes only the imagined writing – of literature is, like drink, one of the substitute satisfactions which remain open to a number of the stunted characters in *Dubliners*, notably Little Chandler and James Duffy.

'An Encounter' might well stand on its own as a quiet and poignant evocation of the first stirrings of dissatisfaction with life and of an attempt at overcoming dissatisfaction which ends, as so much human endeavour ends, with a mixture of moderate successes and sharp disappointments. It is also a vivid presentation of certain areas of Dublin. Its autobiographical basis is found in a real event in the lives of Joyce and his brother Stanislaus which occurred in about 1895 when Joyce was thirteen years old.[1]

The story falls into three parts. The first shows how the Wild West is introduced and translated, tamely enough, into the boys' games. A note of failure is soon struck when the endeavours of all the other boys prove vain against the ever victorious Dillon brothers. But these two, Joe and Leo Dillon, originally showing the most initiative and apparently the strongest, soon drop out of the story. Joe is reported to have a vocation for the priesthood and is not heard of again. For those seeking escape he has become irrelevant; he may even develop to become Father Butler's successor. Following a rebuke from Father Butler, who discovers him with a copy of the *Halfpenny Marvel*, Joe's brother succumbs to authority. The name of that magazine combines two thematic poles of the story—the marvellous world of (imagined) adventures, and the humdrum world of thrift and money. While Leo Dillon is, from the start, frightened and hesitant, the third of the conspirators, who is somewhat condescendingly introduced as 'a boy named Mahony', immediately shows his worth by reassuring the others with the question 'what would Father Butler be doing out at the Pigeon House?'

The central part of the story, concerning the expedition itself, is written in a different tone. The early morning brings a sense of freedom and joyful anticipation, and the narrator feels superior to 'a tramload of business people' who are pulled up the hill by 'docile horses'. He is to enjoy a day's leave from docility and the daily round. Mahony, whose aims do not seem identical with those of the narrator, has brought his catapult along in order 'to have some gas with the birds'. His slangy directness and simplicity of motive form a marked contrast to the other boy's sensitivity and timidity.

The two boys set out alone (towards the south-east – not heading for the Wild West). The spirit of adventure gives way to an interest in the life of Dublin's quays and finally peters out in the sultry afternoon among 'the squalid streets' of Ringsend. The quest

---

[1] Stanislaus Joyce, *My Brother's Keeper*, ed. Richard Ellmann, London and New York, 1958, p. 79.

becomes rather more concrete: they look for a dairy, but fail even in that pursuit. The boys realize that it is too late to carry out the whole project.

The third and last part of the story is devoted to the appearance and the effect on the boys of the strange man with a stick, who comes to them three times. The impression the man leaves is conveyed in such a way that the reader understands more than the narrator does and yet can still share the narrator's sense of something mysterious and vaguely sinister. Most critics have come to refer to the man as 'the pervert', and some have given his deviation a specific label. Whatever the clinical diagnosis of the perversion, it certainly consists in the narrowing down of a vital response to life into the confinement of a few repetitive habits and preoccupations. The perversion does not seem to be acted out: it is chiefly verbal and a matter of the imagination. We do not even always hear the man's exact words; some are quoted indirectly but much of his monologue is summarized. He contradicts himself; words in any case are not entirely to be trusted.[1] There is little real communication, and we may have to allow for a possible distortion due to the boy's agitation. He has already come with some 'confused notion' about green eyes, while the man's green eyes are apt to confuse him even more.

But despite possible distortions the report we get makes it clear that a former feeling of love and desire, a not unusual liking for girls, their 'nice white hands' and 'beautiful soft hair', has been turned into a compulsive fantasy about the whipping of boys. The man's rambling speech terminates in a crescendo of wishful thoughts: '. . . he would give him such a whipping as no boy ever got in this world . . . He described to me how he would whip such a boy as if he were unfolding some elaborate mystery. He would love that, he said, better than anything in this world . . .' (28, 27) Here love has been turned, per-verted, into its opposite. Since love is a door of escape from isolation, a vitalizing contact with another being, the closing of this door is especially pathetic. This man, too, was probably stirred in his youth by the spirit of unruliness. Now he belongs to those who are ranged against it: 'When a boy was rough

---

[1] In '. . . it was reported that he had a vocation for the priesthood. Nevertheless it was true' the assertion of a truth is precisely about something that can never be proved. Only the person who claims to have a vocation can know whether it is true; others must merely judge by outward appearances.

and unruly there was nothing would do him any good but a good sound whipping'. (27, 27)

Some of the fear that this man evokes is due to a dim realization that he embodies what may occur when escape from the restraining and paralysing influences is no longer possible, that he is a spectre of what the boy himself may one day become. Already there are some similarities between them, and the man is in fact eager to stress their both being 'bookworms'. He appears to want to make a convert of the boy. Even his sadism is already present in both boys. Mahony is given to chasing girls, cats or birds. Both of them derive some vicarious satisfaction from 'guessing how many [Leo Dillon] would get at three o'clock from Mr Ryan'. (22, 22) It is significant that the urge is awakened by a preceding failure: 'When we came to the Smoothing Iron we arranged a siege; but it was a failure because you must have at least three'. (22, 22)

The pervert affects the two boys quite differently. The narrator remains fixed, immobile, more and more silent, dares not raise his eyes. He is in a state of seeming revulsion and yet fascination that is not unlike the attitude of the boy in 'The Sisters' as regards Father Flynn. Mahony, on the other hand, extrovert and outspoken, is hardly afraid. He puts a question 'pertly' and boasts of having 'three totties'. His reaction to the man's doings in the middle distance is remarkably nonchalant if, as the reader suspects (and Joyce implied in his letters), the man is really masturbating. Mahony's remarks express surprise rather than shock. As yet the narrator cannot, or will not, face up to this particular aspect of reality.

The return of the pervert brings about a change for all three characters. Mahony simply becomes bored and leaves in order to pursue a cat. The man resumes his monologue, which is no longer about the attractions of girls but dwells on 'the subject of chastising boys'. (This shift of theme and tone before and after sexual release anticipates some of the technique to be richly developed in the 'Nausicaä' chapter of *Ulysses*, which takes place on the beach not far from Ringsend.) The narrator has recourse to a subterfuge, the assumption of other names, which indicates that he feels threatened and that something is happening to his identity.

A character like the elderly man invites speculation as to his significance within a possible symbolic framework. Joyce's emphasis on 'detective stories', 'detection', 'mystery' and a vain attempt to decipher the legend on a Norwegian vessel may well be incitements to deeper probings. Many readings of 'An Encounter' try to explain the old man's significance. He conducts, for example, an initiation for the narrator. The hero goes forth to seek adventures. He is more and more isolated until even his last companion forsakes him; he finds temptation (beautiful girls), terror and instruction, and the 'unfolding [of] some elaborate mystery'. The man then becomes a mystagogue, almost literally so: 'as he *led* me monotonously through the *mystery*'.

The pervert also shows obvious affinities with Father Flynn ('The Sisters') and might be thought of as a debased pseudo-priest. He has been interpreted as a 'symbol of impotent God'.[1] The word 'josser' in Mahony's exclamation can mean God in Pidgin-English (a debased form of English: 'business English'). All these readings may be accepted as aspects of the more general image of the corrupt father. There is an aura of decay about the man with the 'great gaps in his mouth between his yellow teeth', and one critic, who considers that the story describes the spiritual death of a young boy, maintains that the man represents Death itself.[2] Alternatively, he may stand for Ireland, now spiritually dead. His bottle-green eyes would thus be a hint of a particular form of paralysis in Ireland. These readings may help to highlight certain aspects of the story, but they are all the more convincing if they are not overemphasized, if they are recognized as possibilities that enrich the story, but not as a substitute for it or an indispensable key.

Perhaps the most important thing about the man is the aura of mystery that surrounds both him and his words even after we have understood the nature of his perversion and its possible symbolic significance. He seems to contain more than can be rationally grasped. Joyce always refers to him simply as 'a man' or 'the man'. This makes it likely that above all he is meant to portray something generally human – fallible, corrupt, disappointed humanity, not simply someone to despise (as most critics seem to do), but also someone in whom we may recognize ourselves. The man's longing for contact is not solely a homosexual overture, but a very human

[1] Marvin Magalaner and Richard M. Kain, *Joyce: The Man, the Work, the Reputation*, New York, 1956, p. 76.

[2] Sidney Feshbach, 'Death in *An Encounter*', *James Joyce Quarterly*, vol. II, no. 2, Winter, 1965, pp. 82-9.

desire to be accepted and understood. In this, of course, the man's quest fails just as the boy's does: although the narrator recognizes the plea and the offer of affection he is unable to respond to it. His inability is yet another failure in the story.

As opposed to the pervert whom the boys meet without wanting to, the Pigeon House is the desired destination which is never reached. Of it we only know that it is 'out', near the sea, and all we have is its name. The 'pigeon' contained in the name may allude symbolically to the Holy Ghost, whose traditional emblem is the dove (Mat. 3: 16, John 1: 32, etc.). This is in keeping both with Joyce's use of the same motif in his other works, and with the reading of the old man as a perverted God. The quest thus becomes a spiritual one. But while the appearance of the dove in the Scriptures marks a momentous change, there is no corresponding event in the story, only a surrogate of God or of the father is met. Within this theological framework, the predominance in the story of the number three may suggest the Trinity: the three-part structure, the three magazines mentioned, a 'three-master', 'three o'clock', 'three totties', etc. One clear implication is that the spirit for which the Pigeon House stands is of another kind from that taught or incarnated by Father Butler ('what would Father Butler be doing out at the Pigeon House?').

But the pigeon may more simply suggest the bird itself and thus flight and, once more, escape. Mahony's plan, 'to have some gas with the birds', shows that his aims are almost the opposite, but these too remain unfulfilled.

In actual fact the Pigeon House is a conspicuous building far out on Dublin's South Wall, once a hotel, later a fort, and at the time of the story a power house, Dublin's electric light and drainage station. This makes it much more prosaic and less spiritual, but the notions of power and light may still reinforce a theological reading. Or they may simply imply a quest for potency and clarity. It is, however, a fitting irony that, according to the sources,[1] the Pigeon House was named after a certain John Pigeon, who was a civil servant, an employee of Dublin's Ballast Office, and thus a representative of that sort of civic order and official routine from which the

[1] D. A. Chart, *The Story of Dublin*, London, 1907, p. 306; Samuel A. Ossory Fitzpatrick, *Dublin: A Historical and Topographical Account*, London, 1907, p. 148.

boys want to break away. The aim is both more and less than it seems.

There is a similar ambiguity in the associations of Ringsend, the suburb in which the youthful quest comes to a feeble end. The name itself, bringing to mind circular confinement and the inability to escape, is in line with many other phrases expressing movement in a closed circle: the old man's mind 'slowly circling round and round in the same orbit', the magazines being 'circulated secretly', etc. But actually the name Ringsend is derived from two Irish words meaning 'the point of the tide',[1] thus a turning point rather than an impasse. And, historically, Ringsend was Dublin's former place of embarkation to England and the Continent–its chief door of escape. But that was a long time ago. It is 'too late'.

To accept this information as relevant is to accept an historical dimension. The history lesson in the first part of the story may serve as a hint that this acceptance is justified. Ringsend, for example, is associated with Cromwell who landed his army there in 1646: the door of escape once allowed the entrance of the foreign invader. The gospel of love was perverted into the reign of cruelty for which Cromwell is chiefly remembered in Ireland. He thus forms a parallel to the elderly pervert with his delight in whipping boys. There is a puritan sternness in that form of punishment, so intimately connected with the phrase 'in this world' (three times on pp. 28, 27), and promising little love or kindness in the next world.

The Norwegian vessel which repeatedly attracts the boys' attention reminds us of another invasion, that of the Vikings who besieged and conquered, lost and regained Dublin in a long series of historical encounters. Of these the pitched battles and sieges in the Dillons' back garden are a faint and playful echo. Even a cheap tale like *The Apache Chief* is likely to tell its story of conquests in the Wild West, perhaps not so different in kind as Father Butler might think from the conquests that go to make up much of Roman history. The novels of which the pervert avows himself so fond are chiefly historical ones. In their own struggle for independence, largely abortive, the two boys are, on a very small scale, imitating history, and especially a great deal of Irish history. A catapult was

[1] Any edition of *The Post Office Dublin Directory* or *Thom's Directory*, Dublin, under 'Ringsend'. Readers favouring a theological interpretation of the story will welcome the fact that Ringsend is in the parish of St. Mary's.

originally an ancient military engine, a 'stratagem' referred to generalship in war.

Thus the associations of every detail of the story may help to bring a theme into focus. Even the innocuous river Dodder has a record that can be taken as an analogy of the destiny of the protagonists. It too once showed a rebellious spirit and had to be restrained within the banks of an artificial channel.[1]

That the one sentence quoted from Roman history, '*Hardly had the day dawned . . .*', should remain incomplete and mention only a dawning without a subsequent fulfilment, is quite in harmony with the story's theme. It is followed by the unexpected turning up of *The Apache Chief*, just as the boys are to meet with something quite different from the object of their search: a sort of apache. The little school incident thus prefigures the course of the adventure.

A realistic and topographic detail like 'the Vitriol Works', which the boys pass on their way, serves a multiple function, helping to trace the itinerary and contributing to the atmosphere of drabness and depressed city life. Vitriol, moreover, suggests a corrosive influence whose moral equivalent is all too prominent in 'An Encounter' and in other stories in *Dubliners*.

When the boys, at the end of their tether, are described as being left to 'the crumbs of our provisions', the word 'provisions' refers of course to the food they have bought. But the original meaning of the word (Lat. *pro-videre*, to fore-see) is also present: the vision they have foreseen, the Pigeon House, has crumbled. Only fragments are left.

The language of the story is suggestive, yet precise and, on the whole, intricate. It is not the language that a boy of the narrator's age would himself use. There is nothing boyish in the reflective precision of phrases like 'the peaceful odour of Mrs Dillon was prevalent', 'detective stories which were traversed', 'the wall she had escaladed'. This style is fitted to bring out the plight of the elderly man in whom a once youthful vigour has given way to resignation

---

[1] 'There is a tradition that this stream behaved with great perversity when the first bridge was erected there. No sooner was the fabric completed than the waters forsook their old channel, leaving the costly structure high and dry, and, of course, absolutely useless. The peccant river had to be brought back by main force, and narrowly restricted to its present bounds.' Chart, *op. cit.*, p. 305.

and compensation in a fantasy world. The style shows the loss of youthful impetus. There is a note of weary adult disillusionment.

Occasionally, however, something of the freshness of youth and adventure breaks through and the style becomes less distant. Appropriately there is a quickening of the rhythm and a succession of vivid images in the evocation of the early morning, when nature is still full of promise: 'All the branches of the tall trees which lined the mall were gay with little light green leaves and the sunlight slanted through them on to the water'. (21, 21–2) The language itself is gay and lively.

The flexibility of the prose and the skilful handling of indirect quotation are well brought out in the passage describing the boys watching the ships in the harbour. The mood is contemplative, the style leisurely:

'We pleased ourselves with the spectacle of Dublin's commerce – the barges signalled from far away by their curls of woolly smoke, the brown fishing fleet beyond Ringsend, the big white sailing-vessel which was being discharged on the opposite quay'. (22, 23)

The first part of the sentence is general, as though the experience were remembered from a distance in time. The reflective state of mind is expressed by a reflexive verb. The picture of Dublin's commerce is static, a still life, there is hardly any movement. Colours and visual images are prominent, the most vivid of them being conveyed by the phrase 'curls of woolly smoke' – a slight ripple in the prose. There is, significantly, no active verb, even the unloading of the boat is seen as a state rather than as something actually happening. The stillness is interrupted by a sudden impulse, Mahony's remark about running away, and the language correspondingly quickens:

'Mahony said it would be right skit to run away to sea on one of those big ships . . .' (22, 23)

These are Mahony's exact words, quoted indirectly, and by them he is much better characterized than by any description. He is spontaneous, uncomplicated, the stress is on the emotion: 'it would be right skit', and on action, 'to run away'. No time is wasted on description, the most general word will do for 'ship', it is only a means to get away, not something to dwell on. The quick and brisk monosyllables not merely state, but actually express the impulse; they are a stylistic escape, a momentary one, for, as soon as the narrative switches over to 'I', the rhythm slows down again:

An Encounter

'. . . and even I, looking at the high masts, saw, or imagined, the geography which had been scantily dosed to me at school gradually taking substance under my eyes'. (22, 23)

The word 'I' itself, placed as it is between 'even' and a pause, is prolonged, weighty, almost inert. It is separated from its predicate by an interposed phrase, set off by two pauses, as if to indicate that there is a gap between thought and action. Introspection takes over again: 'I . . . saw . . . me . . . under my eyes.' The active verb 'saw' (mental action only), is at once qualified and replaced by 'or imagined', in the manner of the introvert, insecure of himself but perceptive. And it is of course imagination which closes in again to evoke the wonderful image of a mental process. The result is 'substance', not action. The word has religious overtones. A species of transsubstantiation is taking place but it is an earthly one: 'geography'. The words themselves have substance and weight, the style is once again suitably complex.

The narrator's change towards humility, with which the story ends, also finds its appropriate stylistic expression. At the beginning, when Leo Dillon is discovered with a copy of the adventure story, the reaction of the boys is told in a refined vocabulary: 'Everyone's heart palpitated . . . and everyone assumed an innocent face'. The sobering effect of the master's rebuke anticipates the chastening effect of the encounter with the man at the end. The boy has so far shared the inclination, prevalent in his environment, to look down on others for reasons that have little to do with their intrinsic worth or their actions, but have much to do with their social standing and education. He has shown the same contempt for National School boys as that expressed by Father Butler and he is afraid that 'the man would think I was as stupid as Mahony'. This air of superiority can no longer be maintained: the final escape, from the pleading pervert, is accompanied by shame and humiliation. The moral help of Mahony, formerly despised, is now gratefully accepted.

At first a 'paltry stratagem' is necessary, and the style is still elevated: 'Lest I should betray my agitation I delayed a few moments pretending to fix my shoe properly'. But there is a sobering down of the style too when the escape is described. The heart this time no longer 'palpitates': 'I went up the slope calmly but my heart was beating quickly with fear that he would seize me by the ankles.' In distinct contrast to the narrator's concrete fear of being deprived

37

of the ability to move, Mahony is shown to enjoy the free use of his limbs. He is again characterized by running, 'How my heart beat as he came running across the field to me!', and once more Mahony is described by simple monosyllabic words: 'He ran as if to bring me aid.'

As if to indicate a certain complexity and ambiguity, the final sentence seems to hover midway between the simple directness that precedes it and the prevalent more elaborate mode of expression: 'And I was penitent; for in my heart I had always despised him a little.' The statement is straightforward, but there is an air of self-consciousness about it. The heart, which twice before had beaten in physical fact, has again become a metaphor. The language has biblical overtones,[1] and 'penitent' is a religious term. The feeling expressed is not entirely spontaneous, but is connected with the religious elements of the story's background. This reflects a return to familiar things, to school and the catechism, to the bases of the faith in which the boy has been brought up and from whose formality, among other things, the day's outing was to bring a short release. Seen in this light, there is a return to the accustomed order, the opposite of an escape. And yet there has been an initiation of some sort. One of the injunctions of the boy's religion, to grow humble, has been acted out in a genuine experience. In spite of all the failures, some degree of liberation has been achieved.

---

[1] Compare 2 Sam. 6: 16, 'and she despised him in her heart'. Prov. 12: 8 is particularly interesting: 'A man shall be commended according to his wisdom: but he that is of a perverse heart shall be despised.'

Araby

J. S. Atherton

Dubliners was first published on 15 June, 1914; on 27 June the London *New Statesman* printed a review by Gerald Gould saying that 'the little-known Mr James Joyce' was 'a man of genius' who had 'an original outlook, a special method, a complete reliance on his own powers of delineation.' After regretting, first that Joyce displayed 'the cold detachment of an unamiable god', and then that he portrayed 'horrible sordid realities . . . all done quite calmly, quite dispassionately, quite competently', Gould went on to say that 'The best things in the book are "Araby", a wonderful magical study of boyish affection and wounded pride, and "The Dead" . . .' His choice of 'The Dead' as the best of the stories has been endorsed by all critics since, but no one else has placed 'Araby' second. Even the *New Statesman* changed its mind, for in reviewing a new edition on 15 February, 1941, V. S. Pritchett found 'The Dead' and 'Grace' to be the best. Ezra Pound, however, in *The Egoist* on 15 July, 1914, when *A Portrait of the Artist as a Young Man* was being serialized in that periodical, praised the stories in general for the 'clear hard prose' and the 'exclusion of all unnecessary detail', but mentioned only one story by name, saying, '*Araby*, for instance, is much better than a story, it is a vivid waiting'.[1] It seems to me to be emphatically a story and much more than a 'vivid waiting'. Whether it is to be preferred to the other stories or not depends purely on personal taste, but it is worth detailed study from several viewpoints.

The last of the group of stories dealing with childhood, 'Araby'

---

[1] *Literary Essays of Ezra Pound*, ed. T. S. Eliot, London, 1954, p. 400.

was completed by mid-October, 1905, to be followed, in order of writing, by 'Grace', 'Two Gallants', 'A Little Cloud' and 'The Dead'. It appears to have been written specifically to fill a gap which Joyce had noticed in his account of childhood. In the original ten-story version childhood was shown (apart from the boy in 'Counterparts') in only two stories, and neither 'The Sisters' nor 'An Encounter' contained a girl character; indeed the only mention of girls comes from the elderly pervert in 'An Encounter'. Although the stories aimed at presenting a male-dominated Dublin, there should be some account of the dawning of romantic love; even if the heroine has to be as shadowy as the E.C. of *A Portrait of the Artist* or the fictional heroines Pauline and Mercedes whom Stephen daydreams of in that book. And the desire to escape from real Dublin to some exotic place of beauty and freedom, that desire which is only hinted at in the account of the unsuccessful journey to the Pigeon House in 'An Encounter', must be given a more explicit treatment. 'Araby' provides both these features with precision tempered with irony, but accompanied by a suggestion of tenderness and compassionate understanding which is lacking in some of the stories.

'Araby' is typical of Joyce's work in many ways. The first of these that I wish to consider is its partial foundation upon real life. Joyce rarely invented stories, and there are grounds for considering that 'Araby' is based on an actual event in Joyce's childhood.[1] Facing page 80 of Richard Ellmann's *James Joyce* is a reproduction of the programme of an actual bazaar which reads: 'ARABY in DUBLIN Official Catalogue GRAND ORIENTAL FÊTE May 14th to 19th, 1894 in aid of Jervis St. Hospital Admission One Shilling.' This fête was undoubtedly the basis for Joyce's story. He would have been twelve years old at the time and was then, or shortly afterwards, living at 17 Richmond Street North, the house described in the story. Many of the details, such as the provision of a temporary platform to cater for railway passengers to the bazaar, are still verifiable from the files of the Dublin papers. The Christian Brothers' school still stands at the corner of the street, which has altered little from Joyce's time. Some of the houses have been turned into flats but they are still there; so are Richmond Cottages close by, which housed the families whose children Joyce referred to as 'the rough

[1] *Letters*, II, p. III.

tribes from the cottages'. On the other hand, Stanislaus Joyce in *My Brother's Keeper* wrote that, apart from the description of the house, 'The rest of the story of "Araby" is purely imaginary.' Earlier in the same book he claimed that the reference to 'the dark muddy lanes behind the houses, where we ran the gantlet of the rough tribes from the cottages' was to a time before they left Bray, when they 'used to go with other warlike heroes of the same age to engage the enemy, urchins who lived in the lanes behind Martello Terrace'.[1] One is tempted to assume that Stanislaus was wrong and had forgotten the row of slum cottages behind Richmond Street North, but one cannot be quite sure. Joyce usually transformed the actual facts of his past experience when turning them into fiction.

The most obvious alteration is in the family circumstances of the narrator. In 'The Sisters' and 'Araby' he is a young boy living with an apparently childless uncle and aunt: in 1895 James Joyce was living with his parents along with three brothers and six sisters. Richard Ellmann, seeing the story as a report of a real incident, suggests that Joyce's father was 'considerately disguised as an uncle'.[2] It may well be that some desire not to offend his father influenced Joyce at this stage, but I think that he would have resisted this had there not been strong artistic reasons for the change. He wanted the central character to be lonely so as to stand out in contrast to his surroundings. This was necessary if the reader were to be persuaded to sympathize with the boy and condemn his environment. Near relations – parents, brothers and sisters – would have occupied a position in the middle distance between the narrator and his background. Later, when writing *A Portrait of the Artist as a Young Man*, Joyce came across the same problem again and solved it by almost completely eradicating Stanislaus, who was in real life his closest companion.

The uncle in 'Araby' plays an important part in conveying Joyce's idea of Dublin. Joyce saw the city as dominated by unpleasant, selfish, self-satisfied, self-indulgent and self-important father-figures whom the women and children feared and served. The first mention of the uncle comes after a description of the children playing

[1] Stanislaus Joyce, *My Brother's Keeper*, London and New York, 1958, pp. 39, 79.
[2] Ellmann, p. 20. I am indebted to this work and the *Letters* for all the biographical information used.

in the street: 'If my uncle was seen turning the corner we hid in the shadow until we had seen him safely housed.' There is no comment, but the reader's sympathies have been alerted. When the uncle next appears, after the boy's long wait, his entry is described in a way which provides a brilliant example of the creation of atmosphere by carefully selected detail. We are told simply: 'At nine o'clock I heard my uncle's latchkey in the halldoor. I heard him talking to himself and heard the hallstand rocking when it had received the weight of his overcoat. I could interpret these signs.' The effect that is produced, heightened by the 'vivid waiting' which has preceded it, is of a child waiting, listening, and not daring to come out and be seen; and, although no mention has been made of the uncle's intemperance, the reader is led to assume that he has been drinking and that the boy knows this. The aunt is a completely blank character. So much so that when she comes to the boy's rescue she has to be given a kind of literary voltage by having her remark prefaced with the word 'energetically'.

The boy himself is suggested rather than portrayed. He is young, sensitive, usually on good terms with his schoolmaster whose face passed 'from amiability to sternness' when the boy showed in class the results of being under the spell of the magic syllables of 'the word *Araby*'. This obsession with words is, of course, a feature of all the characters who represent Joyce in his work. But this boy is very gentle. His rebellion against his uncle is carried merely to the point of non-acceptance of his uncle's jokes: 'I did not smile.' The brief sentence evokes the picture of a sensitive child, trying to appear dignified, aware of what is expected of him and refusing to comply. The general atmosphere which Joyce conveys of decay and lack of energy shows itself here, as in many other places. Even the description of the children's play, in the third paragraph of the story, succeeds in directing the reader's attention to the sombre houses, the 'feeble lanterns'; and when we are told that 'Our shouts echoed in the silent street' it is the word 'silent' that carries the weight. It is interesting to compare this with a paragraph in chapter IV of Lawrence's *Sons and Lovers* describing a 'wild intense' children's game under a lamp-post, when 'They sounded so perfectly absorbed in the game as their voices came out of the night, that they had the feel of wild creatures singing. It stirred the mother; and she understood when they came in at eight o'clock, ruddy, with brilliant eyes, and quick, passionate speech.' When Joyce's children seem about to burst into energetic movement in 'the career' of the game we are brought into contact with fear of the 'rough tribes' of lower-class children, and confronted with 'the back doors of the dark dripping gardens where odours arose from the ashpits'.

Ezra Pound and others have praised the style of *Dubliners* for its 'exclusion of unnecessary detail', but it is more interesting to study the way in which the stories are crammed with significant, necessary detail. Every detail is intended to carry weight, and repays close study with an intensified appreciation of the stories. The city of Dublin is described in one paragraph as the boy and his aunt 'walked through the flaring streets'. 'Flaring' may seem an oddly chosen word today, but it precisely recalls, to an older reader, the kerosene lamps that lighted the street markets. The sexes are scathingly divided into 'drunken men and bargaining women'. The only goods mentioned as for sale are 'barrels of pigs' cheeks' and even these cheap and unattractive objects have to be protected from the presumably hungry and lawless throng for shopboys 'stood guard' by them. Even the music of Dublin's streets is used to heighten the mockery. The 'nasal chanting' is of O'Donovan Rossa, about whom the popular street ballad[1] describes not, as usually in these ballads, the heroism, but the treachery of the Irish:

> *My curse upon those traitors*
> *Who did our cause betray;*
> *I'd throw a rope about their necks*
> *And drown them in the bay.*

Through this brilliantly evoked ferment of all that is 'most hostile to romance', this crowd of hucksters, drunks, and traitors, the boy imagines himself to be carrying his love as a chalice. We see him as the hero of a romantic tale. The account which follows of how his eyes 'were often full of tears' verges on the sentimental but succeeds in convincing the reader of the sincerity of the boy's misery in his 'confused adoration'.

In the next paragraph we are presented with a background carefully contrasted with the noisy Saturday market as we move into the

---

[1] See *Irish Street Ballads*, collected by Colm O Lochlainn, Dublin and London, 1939, p. 68.

silence of 'the back drawing-room in which the priest had died'. Critics argue as to the extent to which such details in Joyce's work are to be taken as symbolic and meaningful. But there can be no mistaking the effect on the atmosphere of the story of this second reference to the priest who had died, even if we do not have to see in it a symbol of the decay of the church. In a short story such as 'Araby' every detail is intended to carry some contribution towards the total effect: nothing is accidental or put in just to fill up space. And it is typical of Joyce's technique to insert details and leave the reader to pick up the significance if he can. The reader is placed in the situation of an observer of real life: he has to decide the meaning for himself.

Being intensely interested in books, Joyce frequently chooses them as the means to convey suggestions. The books on the floor of the 'waste room behind the kitchen' are of interest here. They include a copy of *The Abbot* by Sir Walter Scott, a book which is relevant to the theme of 'Araby'. Lest I should seem to overemphasize its relevance I will quote from a standard authority, the *Oxford History of English Literature*, Vol. X, by David Jacks: 'The typical Scott hero in spite of his youth and inexperience rapidly becomes a person of great importance . . . Perhaps the most explicit statement of this peculiarity in the career of a Scott hero is found in . . . *The Abbot*, where a youth of no importance whatever suddenly finds himself, as page to the imprisoned Mary Queen of Scots, in a position of vital significance: "Yesterday he was of neither mark nor likelihood, a vagrant boy . . . but now he had become, he knew not why . . . the custodian of some important state secret . . . " '[1] The boy in 'Araby' rejects *The Abbot* and *The Devout Communicant* in favour of *The Memoirs of Vidocq*, a criminal turned detective, simply 'because its leaves were yellow'. At the very beginning of the story he is rejecting religion and romance in favour of a decaying and dubious conformance. Yet I think we are intended to consider him at least in part as the typical Scott hero: he is the boy with his first experience of what it is to be in love, suddenly plunged into 'a position of vital significance'.

Another literary detail which is inserted without comment gives a comic twist to the portrayal of the uncle and aunt. The word Araby reminds the uncle of the Victorian poem 'The Arab's Fare-

[1] *Op. cit.*, p. 189.

well to his Steed' and as the boy leaves the kitchen he is about to recite to his wife its opening lines. They are:

> *My beautiful, my beautiful! that standest meekly by,*
> *With thy proudly arched and glossy neck, and dark and fiery eye!*[1]

The aunt, no doubt, is sitting meekly by; but a further significance may be found in the authorship of the poem, which is by Mrs Caroline Norton, one of the earliest workers for the rights of women, and the original of Meredith's *Diana of the Crossways*. Joyce was interested in women's rights from his student days when he knew Francis Skeffington till the time when he wrote *Finnegans Wake*, where it is sometimes mentioned.

It is frequently said that Joyce had no interest in politics or social matters. This is not true, and one of the features of the stories is their precise presentation of social differences. In a letter to Stanislaus written during the month when he was writing 'Araby', Joyce said 'the chief thing I find in nearly all Russians is a scrupulous instinct for caste'.[2] Only a person who had carefully studied the minutiae of class distinctions in literature and reality could have made such a remark about the great Russian writers; and a student of such matters may find much to interest him in 'Araby'. Its adult characters occupy an oddly intermediate position in the complex order of Anglo-Irish society. They have a 'back drawing-room' and a 'front parlour', which would baffle the U and Non-U experts, but tea can last till eight o'clock and uncle appears to dine in the kitchen in the evening. They are living in a house bigger than they can afford to furnish or use. The servants they cannot afford would have lived in the basement from which the windows lighted the 'area' and needed 'the waste room behind the kitchen'. In a possibly autobiographical story this may be purely factual reporting; but it certainly helps to convey the atmosphere of decadence Joyce aimed at. Even the name of the visitor, Mrs Mercer, seems intended to suggest that this is not the world of romance but the huckster's world where things are haggled for. The entire paragraph about the 'pawnbroker's widow' adds to both aspects of the atmosphere which is being evoked, the sordidness and the suspense.

[1] The poem is included in *Bell's Standard Elocutionist*, London, 1892, p. 309. A copy of this book was in Joyce's library; see Connolly, *The Personal Library of James Joyce*, Buffalo, 1955, p. 8, item 20.   [2] *Letters*, II, p. 106.

The waiting has been for an escape to a far-off land. The theme pervades all the beginning of the book: in 'The Sisters' the boy dreams of 'some land where the customs were strange—in Persia, I thought': in 'An Encounter' after discarding 'the glory of the Wild West' he aims for the ancient point of embarkation from Ireland, the Pigeon House. Now it is Araby; Eveline will fail to leave for Buenos Aires. They are all shown as trapped, and the drama comes from their realization of this.

The boy's journey is described with a precision that is wholly convincing. It is also used to strengthen the air of solitude, of running against the tide, which becomes oppressive. It is just like Joyce to have remembered the price correctly, considered that the child would have expected to go in half price, and to begin the paragraph with 'I could not find any sixpenny entrance', when he finally arrives at his goal. We know where we are: this is accurate narration, perhaps recollection of a real experience. But suddenly we come to the sentence 'I recognized a silence like that which pervades a church after a service' and we remember the dead priest and the yellow leaves, the waste rooms and the general air of decay. Is this a symbol of a decadent religion? Some critics have interpreted it so. The men counting money have always suggested to me the money-changers in the Temple—perhaps this is a personal reaction. But everyone must agree that the total impact of the paragraph is astonishingly successful in conveying an atmosphere of deadness.

The brief reported conversation beginning 'O, I never said such a thing!' sounds very like some of the Epiphanies which Joyce wrote, but it is not included in the collection which has survived.[1] It reveals the entire vacuity of the speakers, but the boy's reaction is not mentioned. He 'looked humbly at the great jars' and lingered apologetically. The rhythm of the sentences is loose and unobtrusive. A final fact has been presented: he has a sixpence and two pennies left. The detail helps to sustain the air of factual reporting. We may idly deduce that his train-fare was fourpence. Then comes the sudden violent reaction, to express which the prose suddenly takes on a forceful rhythm heightened by the alliteration: 'Gazing up into the darkness I saw myself as a creature driven and derided by vanity; and my eyes burned with anguish and anger.'

[1] The most easily available edition is in R. Scholes and R. M. Kain, *The Workshop of Daedalus*, Evanston, 1965, pp. 3-51.

As in all the other stories we have reached a point of stasis at the end; but it differs from the rest in that the stasis is accepted, not with weary resignation but with anger that darkness and negation must be the conclusion. The very fact of the anger suggests that the boy's search for escape will not stop here, although years may have to pass before it can be successful. This is the fitting conclusion to the stories 'representing the period of childhood'. If, as is usually assumed, it is the same boy who is the narrator of all the first three stories, it is at this point we take our leave of him. Perhaps it was to make certain that his readers would see at once that the remaining stories were about other people that Joyce placed next a story about a girl of marriageable age.

Eveline

Clive Hart

Like most of the characters in *Dubliners*, Eveline is oppressed by her environment, and like many others she considers the possibility of escape, but among all the book's principal characters she is the only one who is offered a positive opportunity to leave, an opportunity which she refuses. The interest of the story lies not in the events, but in the reasons for Eveline's failure to accept the offer of salvation. As we shall see, she lacks the courage to go because she has no capacity for love.

Eveline lives in a paralysed and paralysing city in which the last vestiges of happiness crumble away as oppressive houses are built where once there were open fields. There have been changes in Dublin, but they have all led towards a state of immobility and death, and it is ironic that Eveline should think: 'Everything changes. Now she was going to go away like the others, to leave her home.' Eveline's world is becoming increasingly static; in the end she too will abandon the hope of change, will become a part of the stagnation.

The controlling structure of all the main elements of the story—plot, psychological development, imagery—is the opposition between change and no-change, between fevered action and frozen immobility. One of the key concepts which Joyce uses to give expression to this opposition is expressed in the word 'invasion', the idea being present in the first line: 'She sat at the window watching the evening invade the avenue.' Two sorts of invasion are developed in the story. Eveline's environment is subject to two forces: one, the power of paralysis, the other, that of active life. Finally it is the paralysis which wins. As I shall indicate below, although the conflict has been going on for some time, the last struggle is still being fought in the narrative's temporal present.

Dublin has not always been quite so paralysed. Eveline has memories of a happier, freer past which contrasts both with the tedium of the present and with the uncertainty of the future. Joyce chose Eveline's name with care: she is a little postlapsarian Eve, remembering happier days while earning her bread in the sweat of her brow. As a child she lived in circumstances which, for her, represented something approaching Eden. She played in the fields which have now disappeared: ' . . . they seemed to have been rather happy then . . . That was a long time ago.' The evenings, which used to be a time for play, are now one of drudgery, and even in childhood it was evident that happiness was something transient. Her father, wielding his blackthorn stick like an angry god, used to hunt Eveline and her companions in from their play, while the pleasant fields themselves finally ceased to exist when the 'man from Belfast' built houses on them. Now, of course, Eveline's dusty Dublin is again invaded, but, this time, by the forces of life, by the saviour Frank who has come from over the sea to carry her off to a better existence: 'He would save her.'

Joyce allows the opposition to be reflected in the form of the story, which is cast in three main parts: the first, expository, section is an entirely static cogitation on the relationship of past, present, and future; the second is a brief interlude of intense illumination, in which Eveline reasserts her decision to choose life; in the third, her attempt to implement the decision ends in psychological failure. The first section, much the longest, is entirely lacking in action, either physical or psychological; Eveline's thoughts simply succeed one another according to a process of free association. The brief flurry of action in the last makes the victory of the paralysis all the more evident.

The second section, one of the densest and most important passages in the story, begins with a reprise of the opening paragraph: 'Her time was running out but she continued to sit by the window, leaning her head against the window curtain, inhaling the odour of dusty cretonne.' Before the story begins, Eveline has already made her choice to go away with Frank, a choice which is now reasserted as she has a heightened vision, centring on memories of her mother's death, of the futility which surrounds her. The constituent elements of the vision are integrated with some care. First, there is the craziness and subsequent death; second, Eveline's memory of her father, once again represented as a man who repudiates, who hunts people away; third, there is the memory of the man whom on that occasion her father had hunted, the Italian organ-grinder. She must escape from the environment that leads to craziness, and she must leave a father who orders the departure of music and of humanity. The latter point bears directly on Eveline's relationship with Frank, of which her father disapproves. By Joyce's selection of detail, that disapproval is linked with the dismissal of the organ-grinder. Frank loves music – he sings, he took Eveline to see *The Bohemian Girl* – and furthermore he, like the organ-grinder, has come from over the sea: 'Damned Italians! coming over here!' Eveline associates the street organ with the promise she made to her mother, but this emotional nexus is ironically disrupted by the earlier description of the yellowing photograph which 'hung on the wall above the broken harmonium beside the coloured print of the promises made to Blessed Margaret Mary Alacoque'. Her single vision of the death-bed scene indicates very clearly all that Eveline has to contend with.

Already, however, Joyce indicates why Eveline will not, in fact, be able to escape. Paralysis will win because she is not worthy to defeat it. Her inertia is revealed by the excessive value she places on the routine satisfactions of her present existence, and on the pathetically small indications of affection which her father has been prepared to give: 'It was hard work – a hard life – but now that she was about to leave it she did not find it a wholly undesirable life.' '. . . Another day, when their mother was alive, they had all gone for a picnic to the Hill of Howth. She remembered her father putting on her mother's bonnet to make the children laugh.' Despite these memories, Eveline would like to be a 'bohemian girl'. She wants to live, she tells herself, and she hopes to use Frank to help her to do so. Her association with him began without any real personal attachment on her side: 'First of all it had been an excitement for her to have a fellow and then she had begun to like him.' Even now she is emotionally uncommitted: 'He would give her life, perhaps love, too. But she wanted to live.' Frank, in other words, may be useful to her, but she responds only tamely to his much more geniune attachment, an attachment which Joyce indicates in several small ways: he sings 'The Lass that Loves a Sailor', calls her 'Poppens', holds her hand at the quayside. Eveline's feelings, like her life, are shallow. She over-dramatizes her association with Frank, calls it an 'affair' and him her 'lover'; she thinks of herself in pulp-literature terms as 'unspeakably' weary. But most obvious of all is the strong note of falsity in the language of the passage in which she reasserts her choice to leave: 'As she mused the pitiful vision of her mother's life laid its spell on the very quick of her being . . .' Dublin has so paralysed Eveline's emotions that she is unable to love, can think of herself and her situation only by means of a series of tawdry clichés. Finally, in the third section of the story, she is plunged into a state reminiscent of the vision of her dying mother, who had constantly repeated, with 'foolish insistence', a meaningless phrase. Eveline now keeps 'moving her lips in silent fervent prayer'. She asks God to show her the right way, but the only answer she receives is a long, mournful whistle from the boat, which looks to her like a sinister 'black mass', but which, if she were capable of sufficient love and acceptance, might be the means of giving her life. She is reduced to the level of an animal, standing behind the barrier like a sheep in a fold: 'Her eyes gave him no sign of love or farewell or recognition.' As she is loveless, so she must continue to be lifeless.

Joyce emphasizes the basic tension of the story in carefully chosen diction. Eveline's own thoughts are rendered in the third person, but through the medium of diction such as she herself might have used. In the first section there is a general flatness both of vocabulary and of sentence-structure: 'And yet during all those years she had never found out the name of the priest whose yellowing photograph hung on the wall above the broken harmonium beside the coloured print of the promises made to Blessed Margaret Mary Alacoque'. The language of stagnation contrasts, moreover, with the diction associated with life-giving Frank, when Joyce and Eveline use such comparatively strong words as elated, pleasantly confused, excitement, terrible Patagonians. Again, there is a sharp contrast between the diction of the static, early part of the story, and the almost frenzied conclusion of the last struggle.

While choosing diction which will reflect Eveline's character, Joyce at the same time finds words which will function at a further level of significance. The word 'invade' in the opening sentence, while just the sort of hyperbole that a girl like Eveline might be expected to use, is also, for the reader (though not for the character) an indication of the story's theme. A further example of multi-levelled writing is the word 'passed' in the sentence: 'Few people passed.' The simple sense, for Eveline, is that few people walked along the avenue, but the word may, for the reader, hint once again at the theme of the story: few people pass out of the Dublin paralysis, no one in this city is going anywhere. (Later we hear twice about the 'passage' which Frank has booked for Eveline.) A third example of the slightly different sense Eveline's words may have for the girl herself and for the reader occurs in the sentence, 'Perhaps she would never see again those familiar objects from which she had never dreamed of being divided.' Eveline means that it had never occurred to her that she might leave home, but for the reader the word 'dreamed' is an indication of the quality of her imagination, which has never taken her beyond her native city, and of the unreality of her projected flight with Frank. Even her father's friend, the priest, has managed to escape–if only to Australia. Eveline's new awareness of other possibilities in life will always remain at the level of velleities.

Elsewhere, the diction and the choice of significant detail are used to lend an almost subliminal reinforcement to the story's theme. The sense of loneliness and tedium is strengthened by the fact that the man whom Eveline sees walking down the avenue is from 'the *last* house'. Frank's lodgings used to be on the '*main* road'. There is no need to elevate these things to the level of symbols; the connotations of the words 'last' and 'main' are sufficient to help guide the reader's responses. Finally, in this connection, mention might be made of the words 'house' and 'home', which together occur no fewer than eighteen times. Houses are, for Eveline, prisons. By extracting her promise, Eveline's mother condemned her to care for the depressing family home. She has now been offered a choice between the Dublin house and life in Buenos Aires; but she will never leave her prison with its dusty cretonne curtains.

After the Race

Zack Bowen

All of the *Dubliners* stories are concerned with the entrapment of their characters in the moral, social, nationalistic, religious fibres of Dublin life. The revelations or epiphanies of the first three stories deal with the plight of progressively older children, the next four stories with young people, the following four with middle age, and the next three with social institutions. The last story and its revelations comprise a summary.

In the second group of stories, those of adolescence and early adulthood, the entrapment is overtly portrayed in the image of Eveline as a helpless animal behind the bars of the steamship entrance, and in the steamed glasses of Bob Doran as he descends to hear his marital sentence pronounced. In the middle two stories in the group, however, the entrapment is more subtle, though no less real, because it involves mistaken sets of values promulgated by a society which equates morality with social position and ecstasy with money. The deadly sins here are pride, ambition, and covetousness.[1] While the betrayal theme is as prevalent in 'After the Race' as it is in 'Two Gallants', the former story deals with self-betrayal through misguided social values, while the latter compounds self-betrayal with the betrayal of Corley's slavey.

It is not my intention to prove that 'After the Race' is somehow the great undiscovered work of art in *Dubliners*. There is ample evidence that Joyce himself was not satisfied with the story as it was first published in *The Irish Homestead* on 17 December, 1904. Herbert Gorman tells us that even as late as August, 1906, Joyce

---

[1] For an analysis of the sin motif in *Dubliners* see Brewster Ghiselin, 'The Unity of Joyce's *Dubliners*', *Accent*, XVI, Summer 1956, pp. 196-213.

still wanted to revise it, though he never did. One reason frequently given for its not being completely successful is that Joyce is for once dealing with a middle, *nouveau-riche* class of Dublin society with which he had little familiarity. Nevertheless, the portrait of Jimmy Doyle with his exhilaration, aspirations, hopes, fears and guilt is truthful and realistic, even if the significance of the entire piece seems less apparent. Jimmy and his father are out of their depth, uncomfortable, trying desperately to prove themselves in a sphere of activity which they have hitherto only vicariously approached, and in the end Jimmy, at least, though he has made a substantial down payment by the end of the story, seems unwilling to pay the full price demanded for emancipation into another social sphere.

The emancipation is not just from the provincialism of Dublin life, but from the world of butcher shops to the international set, or, more accurately, sports car set. The freedom sought after is not forthcoming for Jimmy any more than it is for Eveline. Like Eveline Jimmy is too imbued with Dublin morality, social customs and upbringing to live the sort of life the Ségouin social circle offers him.

I don't mean to imply that the glittering world into which Jimmy tries to throw himself with such abandon is any less suspect than the glamorous life Ignatius Gallaher conjures up for Little Chandler, or the Eastern splendour of 'Araby'. In 'After the Race', however, Joyce locates the international world in Dublin so close that Jimmy and the elder Doyle can virtually touch it. Their pursuit of a social position in this world is skilfully developed through the images and structural framework of the story into a sort of allegory of Irish history and international relations. It would not be out of place to discuss briefly the structure of the story before proceeding to an analysis of the images and thematic development.

'After the Race' has a conventional three-part scene structure interspersed with two transitional interludes. The major scenes take place in the car, at Ségouin's dinner, and at the party on Farley's yacht, while the interludes, appearing between the major scenes, take place at Jimmy's house and on the street.

Each of the major segments builds to an emotional climax followed by a disillusioning return to normalcy and truth. In the first scene the excitement and hilarity of the race mount to the climax for Jimmy of being seen 'by many of his friends that day in the company of these Continentals'. His triumphant return in the racer to Dublin and 'the profane world of spectators amid nudges and significant looks', is dampened when he and Villona have to get out of the car and walk home: 'They walked northward with a curious feeling of disappointment in the exercise . . .' The episode foreshadows the conclusion of the story. The car and its dizzying speed have led to certain misconceptions on the part of the Doyles, and when the speed and the dizziness finally abate and Jimmy alights again on earth after the giddy ride on the international merry-go-round, there will be little left for him but disappointment and disillusionment.

The interlude between the first and second scenes serves to set the stage for the action to follow by reënkindling Jimmy's anticipation of an evening in the company of his international friends. ('In Jimmy's house this dinner had been pronounced an occasion.') The elder Doyle's naïve enthusiasm for Jimmy's associates contrasts with Villona's for the food which will be served at the dinner. The realities of Villona's concern with the basic essentials as opposed to the Doyles' foolish pursuit of social distinction again prefigures Villona's concluding announcement of daybreak and the harsh light of truth shed on Jimmy's folly.

As the first scene foreshadows the outline and conclusion of the story as well as providing preliminary exposition, the second scene defines the specific nature and method the author will use to develop the action. During the scene the nationalistic elements of the characters come to the fore as Jimmy, feeling 'the buried zeal of his father wake to life within him', engages in heated debate with the Englishman, Routh. This matter will be considered elsewhere in this essay. Once more the high-pitched excitement is dampened, this time by Ségouin, who throws open a window 'significantly'.

The transitional interlude between the dinner and the yacht party again revives the high spirits of the company and contributes to the aura of breathlessness and unreality. We are told, 'That night the city wore the *mask* [italics mine] of a capital.' Dublin was not at that time a capital, any more than was Jimmy an international playboy, but the idea of the masquerade and its attendant illusion permeate the scene, as Mr Doyle's pride and awe of Jimmy and his friends is reaffirmed by the old ticket collector who respectfully addresses Jimmy, 'Fine night, sir!'

After the Race

Armed with the approbation of his elders and a pocketful of money Jimmy is ready to engage in the gaiety and excitement of the last scene, which contains a dizzy dance reminiscent of the auto ride of the first scene; a long impossible-to-remember speech, like the debate of the second scene; toasts to all the nations, thematic of the major motif of the story; and, finally, the card game in which Jimmy can't see his cards clearly, and doesn't know what the stakes are or what he is losing, something we have been led to expect from the mass of evidence which has now accumulated. The climax and the disillusionment following the card game have thus been skilfully prepared for during the balance of the story, and Jimmy's folly comes as more a surprise to him than to the reader, who has come to sense its inevitable conclusion.

Throughout *Dubliners* the narrative point of view, while in the third person, corresponds in tone and phraseology to the state of mind of the central character of each story. Just as the tone of 'Clay' is sweet and naïve, as is Maria, and the tone of 'Counterparts' furious, as is Farrington, so do the breathlessness, excitement, and Scott Fitzgerald-like aura of vapid hilarity and derring-do in the narration of 'After the Race' capture the essence of Jimmy Doyle's mood.[1] Consideration of the image pattern will be combined in the following discussion with an analysis of the thematic development.

We early learn that Jimmy 'divided his time curiously between musical and motoring circles.' The musical-artistic and motoring motifs combine with the international motif to provide the sources of those images which dramatize Jimmy's attempt at emancipation. Young Doyle is trying to escape a mundane middle-class Dublin existence. His intended vehicles to his destination–a place in the international set–are the motor cars of Ségouin and Rivière.

Racing cars are literally the means of bringing the international motoring enthusiasts to Ireland, for they are there to attend and participate in an international auto race. As the autos return from Naas, twenty miles west of Dublin, to Inchicore, a suburb south of Phoenix Park and the Liffey, the international implications of the story and their significance in character delineation become almost

[1] Bernard Huppé has suggested to me that Joyce might in 'After the Race' be attempting a stylistic parody of a turn-of-the-century gentlemen's magazine, in anticipation of such future stylistic parodies as the one in the 'Nausicaä' chapter of *Ulysses*.

immediately apparent with Joyce's description of the machines and the crowd:

'At the crest of the hill at Inchicore sightseers had gathered in clumps to watch the cars careering homeward and through this channel of poverty and inaction the Continent sped its wealth and industry. Now and again the clumps of people raised the cheer of the gratefully oppressed. Their sympathy, however, was for the blue cars – the cars of their friends, the French.' (44, 42)

The cars here, literally embodying the wealth of the Continent with which the Doyles would like to ally themselves, are the means of freeing Jimmy, who represents Ireland, from the yoke of oppression imposed upon him and his country for seven hundred years. The hope that Ségouin and the French will provide this emancipation is reflected in the 'oppressed' Irish sightseers cheering on 'the cars of their friends, the French'. The liberation of the Irish by the French is, of course, not exactly a new idea. The Irish, since the time of the Stuarts and particularly during the days of Wolfe Tone, have regarded the French as prospective emancipators. The failure of the French to free the Irish in the 1690's and in the 1790's leads up to the suspicion that still one hundred years later history will again repeat itself in 'After the Race'.

A French Canadian and a 'huge' Hungarian accompany the Irishman and the Frenchman during the race, and later the party will be joined by an Englishman and an American, thus completing Joyce's miniature League of Nations. It is significant that Jimmy is better acquainted with the impoverished musician, Villona, who shares the rear seat with him, than he is with the other two, though it is Ségouin who will provide the panacea for Jimmy's problems by allowing the Doyles to invest their 'mite' of capital in his new automobile factory.

The elder Doyle, referred to in the local papers as a 'merchant prince', is a self-made man whose social aspirations and future as an industrialist depend to a large extent upon his son, who provides for his father a sort of psychic income because Jimmy is a living example of conspicuous consumption, and his father is 'covertly proud of the excess'. Clearly, Jimmy is the candidate of upper-middle-class Ireland to compete in the moneyed continental set of Europe. Class consciousness and a *nouveau-riche* attitude are apparent in the imagery Joyce uses to set the scene. The word *money* is used nine times in the first four pages of the story, as well as a liberal sprinkling of such terms as *rich, wealth, sum*, etc. The consciousness of wealth gives way to the hopes of the Doyles for further acquisition, as well as increased social stature. Their financial expectations seem infinitely less capable of fulfilment at the end of the evening of hilarity when Jimmy is a heavy loser in the card game. There is about his loss the disturbing impression that maybe it has not all been accidental. There are other evidences that the Doyle money may be going down the drain in the automotive venture as well. We are a little disturbed by the terminology when Joyce tells us that 'Ségouin had *managed* [italics mine] to give the impression that it was by a favour of friendship the mite of Irish money was to be included in the capital of the concern.' Our fears are doubled when we learn that a major factor in the Doyles' investment decision is the nebulous assurance that 'Ségouin had the unmistakable air of wealth'.[1]

Mr Doyle's shrewdness in business is further tempered by his 'eagerness . . . to play fast and loose for the names of great foreign cities have at least this virtue'. He is, in short, out of his depth. His way of dealing with problems of social status, which is really what he and Jimmy are interested in, is not unlike the way his counterpart, the butcher's daughter, Mrs Mooney, deals with moral problems: 'as a cleaver deals with meat'. Mrs Mooney is, however, in her own element and quite comfortable when dealing with Bob Doran, for she is a part of Dublin's entrapment, while Jimmy and vicariously Mr Doyle are attempting in a sense to escape to a world of which they know very little.

The escape is to be fast and furious. The metaphors and images are consistently those of rapture, speed, excitement; the 'trimly built' automobile which will lift the Doyles from the provincialism of Dublin life represents something superhuman, a deliverer: 'The journey laid a magical finger on the genuine pulse of life and gallantly the machinery of human nerves strove to answer the bounding courses of the swift blue animal.'

---

[1] This reading does not represent the only possible construction to be put on Ségouin's motivation. One might very easily infer that Ségouin's car, his Cambridge background, and his rich friends substantiate Mr Doyle's opinion of his wealth, and that possibly Ségouin patronizes Jimmy and will take Doyle's money for his factory, but will not be particularly concerned about what happens to the investment.

The deliverer is properly an object of homage: 'A little knot of people collected on the footpath to pay homage to the snorting motor.' But as the car pulls away, and Jimmy and Villona, curiously disappointed, have to get out and walk, we are led to suspect that the deliverer may not bring the Utopia hoped for.

The aspirations and goals of the protagonist having been established, the scene shifts to Ségouin's dinner. A young Englishman, Routh, becomes the object of a political tirade by Jimmy who feels 'the buried zeal of his father wake to life within him'. Jimmy's roots in Ireland's tradition of militancy cannot be completely extinguished, though they may be submerged or 'modified . . . early', as was the 'advanced' nationalism of the elder Doyle, in order to make money. The motif of the characters as symbols of their respective countries is further augmented by the arrival of Farley, a short fat American whose yacht (an unmistakable sign of an American) becomes the scene of the balance of the narrative. Farley lives up to his Americanism by being taken to the cleaners by the fast-dealing continentals in the best Henry James tradition.

While the hilarity builds to a crescendo Joyce allows the narration, reflecting Jimmy's attitude, to overextend itself, so that it assumes an almost childish storybook atmosphere: 'What merriment! Jimmy took his part with a will; this was seeing life, at least. . . . What jovial fellows! What good company they were!' The gaiety is crowned with an international toast, again overlaid with the implications of façade and extravagance in the narrative, and consequently in Jimmy's thinking: 'They drank, however: it was Bohemian. They drank Ireland, England, France, Hungary, the United States of America.' As the card game commences all the men except Villona play, 'flinging themselves boldly into the adventure'. They drink to the health of the Queen of Hearts and the Queen of Diamonds, symbols of sacrifice and wealth respectively. There are the ominous signs that the sacrifice and the wealth will both be Jimmy's. Young Doyle finally comes to understand that the last 'great' game lies between Routh and Ségouin, as history repeats itself in the struggle between France and England. Jimmy, Ireland, as in the days of Tone, having been an unimportant but involved bystander in the struggle, understands that 'he would lose, of course'. As Routh and England emerge triumphant, Farley and Jimmy, the fat, wealthy American and the Irishman with aspirations are the 'heaviest losers'.

The game finished, there remains only the epiphany which the loss will bring. Some form of epiphany appears in most of the stories of *Dubliners*; however, in 'After the Race' there is an interesting variation on the pattern.

Jimmy doesn't want any sort of light shed on his misdoings. The glimmerings he has of his gross foolishness are enough to make him shrink from having to confront the whole truth: 'He knew that he would regret in the morning but at present he was glad of the rest, glad of the dark stupor that would cover up his folly.' But day has already come; full awareness of the folly is not to be avoided any longer; and the total epiphany of the unwanted truth comes with a Platonistic-Dantesque shaft of light. The most interesting thing about this visualized metaphor of epiphany is that the light frames the figure of Villona, and it is he who announces that the hour of truth is at hand:

'The cabin door opened and he saw the Hungarian standing in a shaft of grey light:

–Daybreak, gentlemen!' (51, 48)

It is only logical to ask, 'Why the Hungarian? What does he have to do with the epiphany?' Jimmy 'divided his time curiously between musical and motoring circles', while Villona is an artist, 'a brilliant pianist–but, unfortunately, very poor'.

It is the musician, Villona, who shares the back seat with Jimmy, who stays at Jimmy's house, and who is the one foreigner with whom Jimmy seems to have something in common. However, Villona's more basic attitudes towards food and survival ('Villona was in good humour because he had had a very satisfactory luncheon'. '. . . the Hungarian . . . was beginning to have a sharp desire for his dinner') contrast strikingly with Jimmy's nebulous aim of social prestige. Attainment of a standing in the continental world will manifest itself for Jimmy in the acquisition of *two* of its most important aspects: money and culture. The cultural aspects, taken for granted by Ségouin and the others, are still the objects of some veneration by Jimmy and his father. Furthermore, the Irish are on an easier footing with the arts, especially music, than they are with international finance. 'His father, therefore, was unusually friendly with Villona and his manner expressed a real respect for foreign accomplishments.'

It is not so surprising, then, that it is Villona, the artist, who finally calls Jimmy, Ireland, from his stupor of folly which predicated its bid for emancipation and freedom on false grounds, for in 'After the Race', as in *A Portrait of the Artist*, it is the artist who will be the priest of the Irish, leading them out of the servitude of their fallacious ways by discovering to them the truth about themselves. The story still does not offer conclusive evidence that the Irish will choose Shem over Shaun (the artist over the man of affairs) any more than they do in *A Portrait*, *Ulysses*, or *Finnegans Wake*. Home-grown artists are still suspect, and Mr Doyle's respect is for 'foreign accomplishments'. But then again, it is no easy thing to forge the uncreated conscience of one's race.

Two Gallants

A. Walton Litz

'Two Gallants' was a late addition to *Dubliners*. When Joyce conceived and wrote the story, during the winter of 1905–6, he had already submitted to the publisher Grant Richards a collection of twelve stories with a symmetrical design. As he explained to his brother Stanislaus, the first part of the collection was devoted to 'stories of [his] childhood' ('The Sisters'–'An Encounter'–'Araby'); the second to 'stories of adolescence' ('Eveline'–'After the Race'–'The Boarding House'); the third to 'stories of mature life' ('Counterparts'–'Clay'–'A Painful Case'); while the last three tales ('Ivy Day in the Committee Room'–'A Mother'–'Grace') were 'stories of public life in Dublin'.[1] On 22 February, 1906, Joyce sent 'Two Gallants' to Grant Richards, with instructions that it 'be inserted between *After the Race* and *The Boarding-House*',[2] and in this position the new story greatly strengthened the second 'aspect' of *Dubliners*, which would otherwise have been the weakest part of the collection. The thirty-year-old Lenehan of 'Two Gallants', poised between the younger Jimmy of 'After the Race' and the rapidly ageing Doran of 'The Boarding House', completes Joyce's gallery of frustrated 'adolescents'; as he wanders back and forth through the city he acts out the plight of young Dublin. 'Two Gallants' provides an essential transition from the tawdry romanticism of 'After the

---

[1] *Letters*, II, p. 111 [September, 1905]. Although the arrangement of the stories within the four sections, as outlined in this letter, differs slightly from the final arrangement, Joyce's correspondence of early 1906 shows that the manuscript submitted to Grant Richards contained the stories in their final order. 'A Little Cloud' and 'The Dead' were added after 'Two Gallants'.

[2] *Ibid.*, p. 130.

Race' to the claustrophobic reality of the later stories. The opening paragraph, with its twilight Dublin of 'gaily coloured' crowds illuminated by pearl-white lamps, sustains the atmosphere of false glamour established in 'After the Race'; but by the end of the story the lamplight has become an agent of harsh realism, revealing the greed and dishonesty which characterize life in 'The Boarding House'.

'Two Gallants' precipitated Joyce's long and frustrating quarrel with his publisher, since the printer refused to set up the story and thereby alerted Grant Richards to the 'controversial' nature of the entire work. In the early stages of his negotiations with Joyce, when a compromise settlement still seemed possible, Grant Richards suggested that 'Two Gallants' could be omitted without too much damage to the collection, 'since originally it did not form part of your book.'[1] Joyce's response to this suggestion leaves no doubt as to his admiration for the story, or its importance in the general design of *Dubliners*:

'I have agreed to omit the troublesome word [bloody] in *Two Gallants*. To omit the story from the book would really be disastrous. It is one of the most important stories in the book. I would rather sacrifice *five* of the other stories (which I could name) than this one. It is the story (after *Ivy Day in the Committee-Room*) which pleases me most. I have shown you that I can concede something to your fears. But you cannot really expect me to mutilate my work!'[2]

Most readers of *Dubliners* would agree with Joyce's judgment. In contrast to the rather thin and stilted 'After the Race', written nearly two years before, 'Two Gallants' shows Joyce in full command of those techniques which made *Dubliners* a turning-point in the development of British fiction. In 'Two Gallants' we find that combination of scrupulously detailed realism and complex symbolism which is the hallmark of Joyce's achievement in the major stories of *Dubliners* and in *A Portrait of the Artist*.

'Two Gallants' is a cold-blooded assault upon the conditions of Irish society. Although in a moment of nostalgia for the attractions of Dublin life Joyce could say that '*Two Gallants*—with the Sunday crowds and the harp in Kildare street and Lenehan—is an Irish

[1] Robert Scholes, 'Grant Richards to James Joyce', *Studies in Bibliography*, XVI, 1963, p. 147 [16 May 1906].
[2] *Letters*, I, p. 62 [20 May 1906].

landscape', he knew full well that he had described that landscape in the 'style of scrupulous meanness' which was his special barrier against sentiment and regret.[1] Like most of the stories which deal with Dubliners of Joyce's own generation, 'Two Gallants' goes beyond a dispassionate rendering of Irish 'paralysis' and treats the theme of active betrayal. Joyce had left Dublin in 1904 feeling that he had been 'betrayed' by many of his contemporaries, and his self-imposed exile in Pola and Trieste only intensified this feeling. When he came to write 'Two Gallants' his sense of personal betrayal was at its height; only a short time before he had given full vent to his bitterness in a letter to his brother Stanislaus.

'For the love of the Lord Christ change my curse-o'-God state of affairs. Give me for Christ' sake a pen and an ink-bottle and some peace of mind and then, by the crucified Jaysus, if I don't sharpen that little pen and dip it into fermented ink and write tiny little sentences about the people who betrayed me send me to hell. After all, there are many ways of betraying people.'[2]

This is the mood in which Joyce wrote his tale of Corley, 'base betrayer', and the 'disciple' Lenehan, and it is a tribute to his art that such personal rancour could be transmuted into analytic irony.

The fundamental irony of 'Two Gallants' is suggested by the title. Corley, with his military bearing, and Lenehan, with his jaunty yachting cap and raincoat 'slung over one shoulder in toreador fashion', are shabby replicas of the gallants of romantic fiction, and their exploitation of the young slavey is an ironic reversal of the conventional pattern of 'gallant' behaviour. But Joyce's irony cuts two ways, and the story strongly implies that the parasitic attitudes of Corley and Lenehan were always a part of the traditional code of gallantry. Stanislaus Joyce believed that 'Two Gallants' was 'inspired by a reference in Guglielmo Ferrero's *Europa giovane* to the relations between Porthos and the wife of a tradesman in *The Three Musketeers*',[3] presumably a reference to that episode in which

[1] *Letters*, II, p. 166 [letter to Stanislaus Joyce, 25 Sept. 1906]. The phrase 'style of scrupulous meanness' was used in a letter to Grant Richards, 5 May 1906 (*ibid.*, p. 134).

[2] *Ibid.*, p. 110 [September 1905].

[3] Ellmann, p. 228 fn. In his *L'Europa giovane* (1898) Ferrero surveyed the differences between the 'Germanic' and 'Latin' temperaments, devoting a long section to the various codes of sexual and romantic love. Joyce may have been drawn to Ferrero's work during 1905-6 by his rather vague interest in Socialist

Porthos uses his status as a 'gallant' to obtain money from the procurator's wife (the wife, dazzled by Porthos' glamour, steals her
husband's money in order to provide him with the trappings of a
gallant). I have not been able to locate this particular passage in
Ferrero's study, but Ferrero's scathing analysis of the essential hypocrisy of the 'militaristic' mind must have struck a responsive chord in
Joyce's imagination. Corley is persistently described in 'militaristic'
terms: the 'son of an inspector of police' who had 'inherited his father's
frame and gait', he 'always stared straight before him as if he were
on parade', and 'was often to be seen walking with policemen in
plain clothes, talking earnestly'. That Joyce considered this al-
liance of 'gallantry' and 'militarism' central to his story may be seen
in his shrewd comments on the prudish reactions of the English
printer:

'Dear Mr Grant Richards, I am sorry you do not tell me why the
printer, who seems to be the barometer of English opinion, refuses
to print *Two Gallants* and makes marks in the margin of *Counterparts*.
Is it the small gold coin in the former story or the code of honour
which the two gallants live by which shocks him? I see nothing
which should shock him in either of these things. His idea of gallantry
has grown up in him (probably) during the reading of the novels
of the elder Dumas and during the performance of romantic plays
which presented to him cavaliers and ladies in full dress. But I am
sure he is willing to modify his fantastic views. I would strongly
recommend to him the chapters wherein Ferrero examines the
moral code of the soldier and (incidentally) of the gallant. But it
would be useless for I am sure that in his heart of hearts he is a
militarist.'[1]

The bracketing of Dumas and Ferrero in this letter would seem to
confirm Stanislaus Joyce's account of the story's origin. In a very
real sense, 'Two Gallants' is an attack upon the stock responses and
illusions of romantic fiction.

But if Joyce's aim, when he began to write 'Two Gallants', was to
expose the hypocrisy of a debased code of gallantry, he soon moved
beyond this theme and wove into his story the leading motifs of
Dubliners: political frustration, economic degradation, and spiritual

---

theory. Writing to Stanislaus on 11 Feb. 1907, Joyce commented in passing that
Ferrero gave him the idea for 'Two Gallants' (*Letters*, II, p. 212).

[1] *Letters*, II, pp. 132-3 [5 May 1906].

paralysis. Next to 'The Dead', 'Two Gallants' is Joyce's most successful synthesis of the major themes of *Dubliners*, and–as we might expect from its place in the process of composition–it is resonant with echoes from the other stories. By the time Joyce came to write 'Two Gallants', 'A Little Cloud', and 'The Dead', he had developed a prose style in which every detail of description contributes both to a local effect and to some larger artistic pattern. Thus the place-names along Lenehan's route, which are supplied with such frequency and precision that his progress can be easily traced on a map of Dublin, contribute a sense of local reality while at the same time emphasizing his lack of 'direction' (like the warm summer air of the opening sentence, Lenehan 'circulates' in the streets). Similarly, the information that Corley 'aspirated the first letter of his name after the manner of Florentines' is both a detail of characterization and a suggestion that the relationship between Corley and the slavey is an ironic inversion of the truly 'gallant' relationship between Dante and Beatrice. In reading 'Two Gallants' we must be alive to every nuance of description and dialogue.

Most critics of 'Two Gallants' agree that the harp in Kildare Street is the central emblem of the story, a point of intersection for the major symbolic motifs.[1]

'They walked along Nassau Street and then turned into Kildare Street. Not far from the porch of the club a harpist stood in the roadway, playing to a little ring of listeners. He plucked at the wires heedlessly, glancing quickly from time to time at the face of each new-comer and from time to time, wearily also, at the sky. His harp too, heedless that her coverings had fallen about her knees, seemed weary alike of the eyes of strangers and of her master's hands. One hand played in the bass the melody of *Silent, O Moyle*, while the other hand careered in the treble after each group of notes. The notes of the air throbbed deep and full.

'The two young men walked up the street without speaking, the mournful music following them. When they reached Stephen's

---

[1] See William T. Noon, *Joyce and Aquinas*, New Haven, 1957, pp. 83-4; W. Y. Tindall, *A Reader's Guide to James Joyce*, London and New York, 1959, pp. 24-5; and especially Robert Boyle, ' "Two Gallants" and "Ivy Day in the Committee Room"', *James Joyce Quarterly*, I, Fall 1963, pp. 3-6. Boyle convincingly demonstrates that the harp – and the verses of Moore's *Silent, O Moyle* – are crucial elements in Joyce's symbolic structure.

Green they crossed the road. Here the noise of trams, the lights and the crowd released them from their silence.' (57-8, 54)

The music of the harpist has no apparent effect on Corley, who moves towards his assignation with a solid tread that has 'something of the conqueror' in it. But the melody haunts the more sensitive Lenehan, and once he is left alone the music breaks through to remind him of his loneliness.

'His gaiety seemed to forsake him, and, as he came by the railings of the Duke's Lawn, he allowed his hand to run along them. The air which the harpist had played began to control his movements. His softly padded feet played the melody while his fingers swept a scale of variations idly along the railings after each group of notes.' (60, 56)

Like the '*Distant Music*' which Gabriel Conroy hears in 'The Dead', the sound of the harp works on Lenehan's subconscious and forces him to act out his own dumb existence. Under his 'idle' hands the harp of passion and patriotism remains mute.

The significance of the harp, however, is not limited to its impact on Lenehan. The harp is a traditional symbol of Ireland's glorious past, and in his personification of the harp Joyce suggests Ireland's modern degradation: 'heedless that her coverings had fallen about her knees, [she] seemed weary alike of the eyes of strangers and of her master's hands'. The melody played on the harp is that of Thomas Moore's 'The Song of Fionnuala', and the unsung words are a gloss on Joyce's story:

> *Silent, O Moyle! be the roar of thy water,*
>   *Break not, ye breezes, your chain of repose,*
> *While, murmuring mournfully, Lir's lonely daughter*
>   *Tells to the night-star her tale of woes.*
> *When shall the swan, her death-note singing,*
>   *Sleep with wings in darkness furled?*
> *When will heaven, its sweet bell ringing,*
>   *Call my spirit from this stormy world?*
>
> *Sadly, O Moyle, to thy winter-wave weeping,*
>   *Fate bids me languish long ages away;*
> *Yet still in her darkness doth Erin lie sleeping,*
>   *Still doth the pure light its dawning delay.*

When will that day-star, mildly springing,
Warm our isle with peace and love?
When will heaven, its sweet bell ringing,
Call my spirit to the fields above?

In his *Irish Melodies* Moore provided a note on the song's legendary background: 'Fionnuala, the daughter of Lir, was by some super-natural power transformed into a swan, and condemned to wander, for many hundred years, over certain lakes and rivers in Ireland, till the coming of Christianity; when the first sound of the mass bell was to be the signal of her release.'[1] Lir was the sea in Irish legend, and the plight of 'Lir's lonely daughter'–the plight of Ireland–may be linked to that of the servant girl, whose 'blue dress' and 'white sailor hat' remind us of the sea. Like the harp, the servant girl must submit to the 'eyes of strangers' and obey 'her master's hands'. We should also have in mind a tradition recounted in the opening stanza of another of Moore's *Irish Melodies*, 'The Origin of the Harp':

'Tis believ'd that this Harp, which I wake now for thee,
Was a Siren of old, who sung under the sea,
And who often, at eve, thro' the bright waters rov'd,
To meet on the green shore a youth whom she lov'd.

The sordid circumstances of the slavey's affair with Corley are placed in tragic perspective by the romantic and patriotic legends associated with the Irish harp.

Clearly the young slavey and the harp in Kildare Street represent Ireland's contemporary subjugation, her lack of political independence and national pride. But these symbolic values would have little impact on our imaginations if the human situation were not so powerfully presented. The servant girl, with her 'frank rude health' and 'unabashed blue eyes', stands in ironic contrast to Lenehan. His 'servility' has been a matter of choice, hers was thrust upon her by economic necessity. In her we see the peasant virtues–which Joyce, like Yeats, admired–corrupted by the pressures of Dublin life. She thinks of Corley as a 'gallant' belonging to another social class, one who could have 'girls off the South Circular', and Corley plays upon this social advantage in his exploitation of her. On one level the story is clearly susceptible to a Marxist interpretation, and

[1] Joyce was well acquainted with the legend. See Appendix, p. 174.

it is this grounding in social and economic reality which makes Joyce's elaborate symbolic performances possible. The sovereign which Corley holds up for Lenehan's admiration at the end of the story is, of course, a complex symbol, but it is first and most importantly a gold coin. Just as in 'The Boarding House' Joyce never allows the theological connotations of the word 'reparation' to dominate its economic meaning, so in 'Two Gallants' he keeps our attention fixed on the shabby social and economic circumstances of Dublin life.

Another important motif in 'Two Gallants' is that of religious 'betrayal'. As Florence L. Walzl has pointed out, the story abounds in religious and liturgical references.[1] Lenehan's thrice-repeated 'That takes the biscuit!' is not only a characteristic speech-pattern (he uses the same phrase in *Ulysses*) but a reference to the Sacred Host. His lonely meal may be an ironic inversion of the Last Supper, and at the end of the story he is presented to us as Corley's 'disciple'. The mass bell of Moore's song never rings. The colours of the slavey's dress are those of the Virgin. These references, and many less obvious ones explored by Miss Walzl, cannot be denied. Just as the futile pilgrimage of the little boy in 'Araby' is given religious significance through a series of liturgical references, so the betrayal of the slavey takes on religious overtones. Communion among men has been broken in Dublin; what should have been a Love Feast has become a solitary and furtive meal. In their daily betrayals of themselves and others the citizens of Dublin are acknowledging their spiritual paralysis.

It is these carefully developed symbolic motifs which give 'Two Gallants' that 'unity of effect' we demand of a great short story. By deliberately withholding from the reader until his last paragraph the true purpose of Corley's mission, Joyce ran the danger of constructing a suspense story which would depend, in the manner of Maupassant or even O. Henry, upon a 'trick' ending. Certainly most readers of 'Two Gallants' are shocked, upon first reading, by the revelation of the 'small gold coin'. But after this initial surprise has been assimilated the reader realizes that the dénouement was inevitable, that the entire story tends towards this shocking conclusion. The gold coin – probably stolen, like the cigars, from the servant

[1] Florence L. Walzl, 'Symbolism in Joyce's "Two Gallants"', *James Joyce Quarterly*, II, Winter 1965, pp. 73-81.

girl's employer—is a final symbol of debased 'gallantry', but it is also a fitting climax to the related motifs of Ireland's political, economic, and spiritual degradation. It is a true epiphany, a showing forth of hidden reality, and like all Joyce's epiphanies it is wholly dependent upon its context.

The symbolic motifs in 'Two Gallants' which we have been discussing may appear to be obvious and even mechanical but within the living form of the story they are unobtrusive. Much more obvious upon first reading are Joyce's careful modulations of mood and atmosphere. The story opens with a description of the Sunday streets which matches the jaunty mood of the two gallants.

'The grey warm evening of August had descended upon the city and a mild warm air, a memory of summer, circulated in the streets. The streets, shuttered for the repose of Sunday, swarmed with a gaily coloured crowd. Like illumined pearls the lamps shone from the summits of their tall poles upon the living texture below which, changing shape and hue unceasingly, sent up into the warm grey evening air an unchanging, unceasing murmur.' (52, 49)

Soon, however, the appearance of a 'large faint moon circled with a double halo' brings the thought of rain to Lenehan, and perhaps of something more: 'He watched earnestly the passing of the grey web of twilight across its face.' As the twilight fades into darkness, and the moon is obscured by rain-clouds, Lenehan's thoughts darken. After Corley has departed with the girl his mind turns in upon itself.

'He was tired of knocking about, of pulling the devil by the tail, of shifts and intrigues. He would be thirty-one in November. Would he never get a good job? Would he never have a home of his own? He thought how pleasant it would be to have a warm fire to sit by and a good dinner to sit down to. He had walked the streets long enough with friends and with girls. He knew what those friends were worth: he knew the girls too. Experience had embittered his heart against the world. But all hope had not left him. He felt better after having eaten than he had felt before, less weary of his life, less vanquished in spirit. He might yet be able to settle down in some snug corner and live happily if he could only come across some good simple-minded girl with a little of the ready.' (62, 57-8)

But Lenehan cannot escape from the aimless life of the streets, which is all we see of Dublin in this story; and by the time ten o'clock arrives his earlier jauntiness has given way to anxiety and suspicion. The moon of illusion has vanished. Perhaps, he thinks, Corley will betray him as he has betrayed the girl. As the first drops of rain begin to fall Lenehan witnesses Corley's return, but by now he feels that his own sense of failure must be assuaged through Corley's success. The old tone of camaraderie is gone, and a 'note of menace' enters his voice as he demands an answer: 'Did you try her?'

These parallels between Lenehan's moods and the changing tones of Joyce's 'Irish landscape' should remind us that 'Two Gallants' is, above all else, Lenehan's story. We see Corley only from the outside; we know what he says and does, and how he looks, but not how he feels. It is this external presentation which makes Corley such a menacing and inhuman figure, the true embodiment of a perverted code of gallantry. In the case of Lenehan, however, we are given a record of his inner life, and our sympathy is inevitably elicited by the pathetic aspects of his experience. As he whiles away the time during Corley's absence, we begin to share his prurient interest in Corley's affair, until at the end of the story we are as anxious as Lenehan to know the truth: 'Did it come off? . . . Did you try her?' And when the 'small gold coin' is revealed, we are likely to feel–to the extent of our interest in Corley's mission–that we too have been his 'disciples'. In 'Two Gallants' Joyce shows as little pity for his readers as he does for his characters.

The Boarding House

Nathan Halper

I

This is not a difficult story. Although much of it is told in flashbacks and the point of view keeps shifting from one person to another, it is clear what is happening. We have no questions: in the story itself, each actor understands what he or she is doing and shares with the reader a knowledge and understanding of what the others are up to.

As far as I know, there have been no articles about it. It has usually been discussed only when a writer is doing each of the fifteen stories, and, when this is the case, the comments on 'The Boarding House' are among the briefest. William Tindall has three paragraphs, part of which he uses to say that, though it deals with guile, the story is so 'guileless' that 'comment seems unnecessary'.

The only one to give it special attention is James S. Atherton. Near the end of a general essay on *Dubliners*, he takes two pages to show how the story is constructed. He chose it 'mainly because this is an average sort of story which nobody has ever said was better or worse than the other stories in *Dubliners*'.

If it was written by Joyce, there should be things to explicate. But this story speaks for itself, doing it so efficiently that the commentators have been dissuaded from looking for the things that they look for in the others. Yet, on the other hand, if it has no need of critics, of symbols or parallels, no need of 'readings' to bring it to its fulfilment, that is in some ways an advantage. Here is a place where it is safe to speculate.

'The Boarding House' was written in Trieste where Joyce had

moved in March, 1905. On 12 July, he wrote to Stanislaus. 'I send you tomorrow the fifth story of "Dubliners" that is, "The Boarding House"... I have also written the sixth story "Counterparts"... I am uncommonly well pleased with these stories.' One week later, speaking of the 'torrid weather', he confirms that they were done in the same period. 'Many of the frigidities of *The Boarding-House* and *Counterparts* were written while the sweat streamed down my face on to the handkerchief which protected my collar.' Indeed, there are links between them – a group of clerks who 'share in common tastes'; *artistes* from the music hall; Jack Mooney with his fists (his father with a cleaver); Farrington with his 'spasms of rage'. Joyce tends to shy away from the criminal or violent. These stories are as near as he comes to it.

In the early scheme for the book 'The Boarding House' was the first of three stories about adolescence. Bob Doran, its protagonist, is thirty-four or five. He is one of the 'young men'. This phrase is used half a dozen times in two paragraphs, but it is only later, when Mrs Mooney reviews how she is going to handle him, that his actual years are mentioned. Then, in a couple of seconds, she returns to thinking of Doran as a 'serious young man'. Meanwhile, he himself is thinking that he is no longer young. This is intentional. The ambiguities – unseasonable immaturity, tenacious adolescence, a retarded marriage – are among the features of Joyce's picture of Dublin.

It is more puzzling that he follows the story by 'After the Race' and 'Eveline'. The categories get older and yet, in those stories, the people are progressively younger. In the event, however, this order did not last. A few weeks later, when he offered his book to Grant Richards, the publisher, they were in the present sequence. Since his tale of Little Chandler had not as yet been written, 'The Boarding House' was followed by its sibling, 'Counterparts'.

Though they are a pair, these belong in different age-groups. The 'boys' in 'Counterparts' are at a later stage than Mrs Mooney's young men. They are more conscious of 'indignities'; their violence is more embittered. Joyce still cannot bring himself to show this in action, but it is closer to the surface, more vicious. The sex is more sordid, the drinking more sodden. Farrington is a promise of Bob Doran's future.

There is a hint of a similar prognosis in 'The Boarding House'. Polly will resemble her mother. Like old Mooney, her father, Doran

73

will go 'to the devil'. He reappears in *Ulysses*: 'the lowest blackguard in Dublin when under the influence'. Paddy Leonard, who knows the bobby, saves him from being arrested, and it is fitting that Paddy should figure in 'Counterparts'. We should be careful about apply- ing what was written at another time and in another book, but in this instance what we are told in *Ulysses* is no more than a statement of what has been long implicit.

Early in 1906 there were two more stories, 'Two Gallants' and 'A Little Cloud'. No longer the first of three, 'The Boarding House' became the last of four about adolescence. In the next two, the protagonists are married. Little Chandler, Farrington . . . these are examples of 'maturity'. The story of Doran, of how he gets married, is the bridge that leads to it. In this arrangement, 'The Boarding House' is paired with 'Two Gallants'. This is not a radical change. Like the men in 'Counterparts', the gallants are raffish, but the new combination allows different aspects to be emphasized.

Lenehan is thirty. He and Corley are introduced to the reader as two young men. These are tales of adventure, in each of which the hero woos and wins the maiden. This is a traditional episode, a favourite in the story-teller's account of his gentle warriors.

In one, we have the title 'Two Gallants'. When Mrs Mooney, in the other, hears her daughter's confession, she tries not to receive it 'in too cavalier a fashion'. Bob Doran is a 'man of honour': 'there must be reparation', there is 'one reparation' for 'the loss of her daughter's honour'. Bob is aware of his 'sense of honour', 'reparation must be made'.

Corley walks 'as if . . . on parade'. Jack Mooney, who works for a commission agent in Fleet Street, is 'fond of using soldiers' obscen- ities'. When he meets Doran, they 'salute'. Mr Mooney, the father, has to 'enlist' as a bailiff.

Mrs Mooney 'kept her own counsel', 'when she judged it to be the right moment, Mrs Mooney intervened', 'she was sure she would win', 'she felt sure she would win'.

The writer is pedantic. A student of words and forgotten meanings, Joyce makes use of terms – 'loophole' or 'belfry' – which, on the surface, are peaceable, yet which originally had meanings connected with warfare. There are also the churches. From her window, Mrs Mooney looks out on the circus in front of St George's Church. George – the hero on horseback, who slew the dragon and rescued a princess – is Church of Ireland. Mrs Mooney cannot use him. If she wants a 'short twelve', she goes to Marlborough Street. Marlborough was a soldier. Although other churches are nearer, it is Marlborough she uses.

Jack Mooney has a 'bulldog face', and Lenehan is 'a leech'. At the same time that Joyce was writing these stories, he was working on *Stephen Hero* in which he speaks of the 'importunate devil within him whose appetite was on edge for the farcical'. Joyce tries to mask him under phrases that are commonplace, but this 'devil' is in *Dubliners*. 'Leech' and 'bulldog' are words which express the attribute of being unyielding: constant, resolute, steadfast.

Many virtues are mentioned but, even when he is not farcical, Joyce uses them in such a way that they are mocked or sullied. 'Diligence' and 'industry' are the appropriate qualities for a serious young man who suspects he has 'been had' while having no idea what on earth he can do about it except go along. 'Good' is used to mean a 'good thing', an accessible *artiste*. 'Hospitality', like 'honour', is a tool in the hands of Mrs Mooney.

Mrs Mooney shows 'tolerance'. She and Polly are 'frank', Mrs Mooney in questions, the daughter in answers. Polly looks like 'a little perverse madonna'. 'Wise' and 'innocence' combine, only to tarnish each other. In her 'wise innocence', Polly Mooney has 'divined' what her mother is doing, and there is a lascivious hint in the statement 'she had made a clean breast of it'.

The story, Stanislaus says, was suggested 'by the rude and fluent remarks about his landlady and her daughter made by a little Cockney', the other English teacher in the Berlitz school in Trieste when Joyce first arrived there. The teacher may be present in the story as the 'little Londoner' whom Jack Mooney threatened because of a 'free allusion' to Polly. Joyce found his other characters in Dublin – the implications are those of Dublin.

The house is given a Dublin location in Hardwicke Street. Since one can see the circus in front of St George's Church, it must be close to Hardwicke Place, which is on the other side of Dorset Street from Eccles Street, and not far from Bloom at No. 7. Bloom was not yet in Joyce's mind, but when he came to *Ulysses*, he took care to mention that the Mooney boarding house used to be in Hardwicke Street. When Bloom and Stephen walk from Nighttown to Eccles Street, they pass the circus.

One can imagine the 'rude and fluent remarks'. The young lodgers refer to Mrs Mooney as *The Madam*. (She took Polly home 'to do housework'.) 'As Polly was very lively the intention was to give her the run of the young men', the 'house was beginning to get a certain fame'. In fact the mother's 'tolerance' suggests *maison de tolérance*. When Joyce, in *Finnegans Wake*, puns on the names of these stories, this is a 'boardelhouse', and it is likely that, when he used the title, he already had in mind a similar pun on 'bawdy house'.

In the 'Cyclops' chapter of *Ulysses*, the Narrator alludes to the 'old prostitute of a mother procuring rooms to street couples'. Since the speaker is scurrilous, this may or may not be true, but at any rate, it is not mentioned in 'The Boarding House'. But, even there, in a metaphorical sense, the place is a brothel. Mrs Mooney is a Madam who makes a body available, lets it be an enticement. If a chap is eligible, she allows the body to be used, but insists on payment.

There are pretensions. She does not use a parish church. (Marlborough Street is the cathedral.) There are lace curtains, and the parlour is the 'front drawing-room'.

There are appearances. Although what the mother is doing could not 'be misunderstood', there is 'no open understanding'. When they speak to each other, the two women are 'awkward'. The word is used for each of them. Mrs Mooney who does not wish 'to seem to have connived', is 'made awkward'. Polly does 'not wish it to be thought' that she sees 'the intention' behind the other's tolerance.

If anybody makes a 'free allusion' to her, Jack Mooney is there to correct him. ('He'd bloody well put his teeth down his throat.') There are certain decencies. Young Mooney will maintain them.

Mrs Mooney sees the matter in its basic monetary terms. Bob Doran has 'a good screw', 'and she suspected he had a bit of stuff put by'. 'She did not think he would face publicity', in which, as he realizes, she proves to be right. If he does not marry, the affair will be talked of: 'his employer would be certain to hear of it,' 'all his long years of service gone for nothing!', 'Dublin is such a small city: everyone knows everyone else's business'.

The word 'business' is used to mean private affairs, but the private affairs boil down to money and business – the word becoming a figure of speech for itself. When, however, she thinks of what she

76

will say to him, the money is minimized, the sentiment prettified: the language in which she dresses it becomes more formal. There is, clearly, 'only one reparation . . . for the loss of her daughter's honour'. She does not wish it to seem as if she has connived, while he does not wish it to look as if he has no dignity, but each knows what the other is doing, and that the other knows it. The pressures, that is, are exerted in a mutual framework of propriety.

II

As Joyce wrote to Stanislaus, the first three stories are of 'my childhood'. They are told in the first person, while the others are in the third, but it has been suggested that the people in some of these later stories nevertheless have a relationship to Joyce. They are perhaps hypotheses, projections into the future, of the person he would have become if he had stayed in Dublin. Lenehan, Little Chandler, Duffy and Gabriel Conroy have been offered as examples. I do not see why no one has yet mentioned Doran.

When Joyce met Nora, she was working in Finn's Hotel, which Ellmann has described as a 'slightly exalted rooming-house'. Nora was no Polly, neither had Joyce met her mother, but when he wrote of Doran, he had first-hand knowledge of his thoughts.

'There was her disreputable father', 'she *was* a little vulgar; sometimes she said *I seen*'; 'he could imagine his friends talking of the affair and laughing'; 'the family would look down on her'. Or, perhaps, 'he could not make up his mind whether to like or despise her for what she had done'.

Doran, as we have noted, is thirty-four or five. When Joyce wrote this story, he was twenty-three, and had been twenty-two when he left Dublin with Nora. But Doran has been employed for the last thirteen years. (Joyce makes a point of the number.) He was therefore twenty-one or two when he started the job. And, in a few particulars, he resembles the Joyce of that age. 'He had sown his wild oats, of course; he had boasted of his free-thinking and denied the existence of God to his companions.'

Like Doran, Joyce might wonder. 'What could he do now but marry her or run away? He could not brazen it out.' And yet, unlike Doran, it was not the girl he objected to but the institution of marriage. It was only later, when he came to write 'The Dead', that he dealt with the possibility of their having married and stayed.

A letter from Trieste shows how he shared the other's fear about his job. 'The slightest disapproval on the part of my genteel pupils would be sufficient to obtain for me dismissal and with my "immorality" . . . I should find it next to impossible to get anything to do here.' As an expectant parent, his worries were not only financial. (His son was born two weeks after he finished the story.) And there were the usual problems of any youthful couple. He kept trying to justify the step that they had taken, saying 'like everything else that I have done in my life it was an experiment'. He follows the statement with a list of the things he has accomplished. 'I do not think that I have wasted my time.'

On a different level, there were pompous pronouncements. 'The struggle against the conventions in which I am at present involved.' 'You know', he wrote to his brother, 'that Nora is incapable of any of the deceits which pass for current morality'. When he heard the remark about a landlady and her daughter, he used it, perhaps consciously, as a way to reassure himself.

Here is Polly Mooney, of an age with Nora. Joyce could say of the latter 'I admire her and I love her and I trust her', 'you know, of course, what a high esteem I have for her', but she was atypical. Polly, by contrast, is the sort of girl one would meet in Dublin.

What is Doran's link with Polly? When her candle went out she went into his room. He remembers 'the touch of her hand and his delirium'. But–the 'delirium passes' and, even while it lasted, it appears to have lacked intensity. Polly is 'lively', but this means no more than that she is flirtatious. When she thinks of sex, it is connected with 'revery', 'hopes and visions of the future', and she has 'secret amiable memories'. He, however, felt the delirium, and she has her memories, for both of which he will pay.

Here is Mrs Mooney: an 'imposing woman', one who imposes. Being acquisitive, she is 'quite able to keep things to herself'.

This is the sort of pressure Joyce would have suffered in Dublin. It is not a question there of having a meaningful relationship. The important thing is marriage: the words, the document. Far from being a sacrament, it is, rather, a manifestation of the simony, the surrender of the spiritual to the temporal, mentioned on the first page of *Dubliners*.

There is also Doran, who is the first in time of those bleached and enervated Joyces who begin to appear in the book. In terms of the situation, he is also the most relevant. The other stories are saying, 'It was the right thing to leave Dublin.' In this one, Joyce is saying: 'It was right to leave it with Nora.'

The story is self-sufficient, needing no reference to Joyce's life, but, if a reference is there, the reader is not obliged to close his eyes to it. This applies equally to other parallels. In 1944, Richard Levin and Charles Shattuck published an essay, 'First Flight to Ithaca', in which they suggested that before Joyce used the *Odyssey* in *Ulysses*, he had already done so in *Dubliners*. Their study of 'The Boarding House' is predictably their briefest. They say it mirrors the interlude of Aphrodite and Ares, the song Demodocus sang in the palace of Alcinuous.

They see Homer as a framework, a device that gave Joyce some details of plot and characterization. Polly – 'light soft hair' – is 'Aphrodite of the fair crown'. Bob – who has not shaved in a few days – has a red beard like Ares. Hephaestus, Aphrodite's husband, discovers that they are lovers and builds a net that catches them. Mrs Mooney – Hephaestus – is Aphrodite's closest relative, in whose house – as it was in his – the affair is happening. Jack Mooney is Poseidon. Each is a lover of horses; each shows a bias in favour of the goddess.

I will not discuss the theory in general, but, in this particular story, I would go further than they do. Joyce *is* 'on edge for the farcical'. Consider Polly's brother, who, being Poseidon, the god of oceans, works in Fleet Street. As the god of fishes, he has two bottles of Bass. We have noticed martial allusions, and the story is about Ares. It may also be significant that there is a circus near the boarding house. Joyce has been careful to give the home this location. The temple of Venus was near the Circus Maximus.

'All the lodgers in the house knew something of the affair; details had been invented by some.' In *Ulysses*, one has an account of Polly naked on the 'landings'. Landing – naked from the sea – suggests the Birth of Venus. The combing-jacket she wears when she calls on Doran may be a further allusion to the combers, or waves. The young bachelor lodgers are the bachelor gods, 'rakish' and 'loud-mouthed'. ('Laughter unquenchable rose among the blessed gods.') They are merely 'passing the time away: none of them meant business'. But, like Apollo and Hermes, they may not be entirely averse to being there in place of Ares.

These identifications, much as they may amuse the writer, have a serious purpose. Joyce uses the world of Homer as a comment on his own. Things are different in Dublin, but before he shows the difference, he must be able to show that, up to a point, the situations are similar: they have enough in common to provide a basis for comparison.

Sometimes a link is simple. Aphrodite is a 'shameless girl', while Polly sings: '*I'm a . . . naughty girl.*' But he does not always find so uncomplicated an equivalent. This is partly from choice. He wants something to crackle under the surface sobriety, and so he has his games. But if the links are funny, this is incidental; the important thing is that they are there. Once this is established, we may go on to examine the difference.

Mrs Mooney is Hephaestus. It does not matter that he is a husband or lame. Neither is germane to the motif. 'Hephaestus strewed his snares all about the posts of the bed.' She sets a trap: a trap connected with a bed. The significant contrasts are those related to the working-out of the theme.

Hephaestus feels he is 'dishonoured', which she merely pretends to be. 'Wild rage gat hold of him, and he cried terribly', but she counts 'all her cards'. He is trying to break an unbearable relationship, but she is out to create one. He wants his 'gifts of wooing', because to him they are a symbol of marriage, but Mrs Mooney is more venal. Marriage for her, even a poor one, represents material benefit.

In Homer the exposure is literal, physical, but in Dublin it takes the form of publicity. Only the threat of it is needed. Even this is not spoken, merely implied.

Ares is subject to 'the fine of the adulterer'. When he promises to pay, they are released from the trap and he goes to Thrace. Doran longs 'to ascend through the roof and fly away to another country', but it is when he pays the penalty that he is thoroughly, irrevocably, in the trap.

One may go further. The Mooneys have a reunion in the 'front drawing-room', and there is a similar gathering in the palace of Alcinuous. Both offer music and dancing. After describing it, Joyce gets into his story: Demodocus begins his song.

We may go even further. Homer says Odysseus was there: he 'listened and was glad at heart'. But, in Joyce's version, he is an active character. (Doran in Gaelic means an exile or stranger.) Bob Doran is Odysseus.

Like the hero of 'The Boarding House', Odysseus is an older man, with a good position. Nausicaa is Polly. In Book VI of the *Odyssey*, Nausicaa, with her fair tresses, sings and dreams of getting a husband. The friendship between them starts when she is doing some washing. She gives him meat and drink. (Polly 'warmed up his dinner . . . there was sure to be a little tumbler of punch'.) When the father is mentioned it is usually in connection either with drinking wine or mixing it. (This is old Mooney.) The mother is dominant; she notices; she wonders about her daughter's relation with Odysseus. Nausicaa's brother, Laodamas, is 'the foremost' in boxing, while Jack Mooney is 'handy with the mits'.

Nausicaa and her family would like the lodger to marry her, but nobody attempts to trick him. They help him: give him gifts, according to the code of the generous host. He, for his part, makes no effort to sleep with the landlady's daughter.

Back to 'The Boarding House': in Demodocus' song the bed is the centre of the stage, but here it is brought on the scene only as the play is ending. It is the woman–(as in the *Wake* or *Ulysses*)–who has the final moments. Polly sits on the bed, refreshes her eyes, readjusts a hairpin, then goes back to the bed again. 'She regarded the pillows for a long time and the sight of them awakened in her mind secret amiable memories. She rested the nape of her neck against the cool iron bed-rail and'–(like Molly Bloom)–'fell into a revery.'

Polly is Nausicaa, but she is going to be married. As the wife of Odysseus, she corresponds to Penelope.

'She waited on patiently . . .'

'Mr Doran wants to speak to you.'

After almost twenty years, she is going to get Odysseus.

'Then'–(the last line) – 'she remembered what she had been waiting for'.

Joyce is writing a story. The Joyce who is writing is a model for the story. As another, he takes an adventure in Homer. In it there is an interlude during which a song is heard. This is another model: there are boxes in boxes. His story, 'The Boarding House', is a travesty of all of them.

The song is cynical, a parody in itself. The gods are not godly, are not even exemplary human beings, but they have *joie de vivre* and lack hypocrisy. Joyce removes the zest, and adds a little hypocrisy. The song is an entertainment, the situation farcical. In the story – it is happening. This is Dublin. They are people. This is the way they exist.

There is another box. Hephaestus makes two statements: 'Come hither', he says to the gods as he calls them to the spectacle. 'Come hither, that ye may see a mirthful thing and a cruel.' Joyce makes it both more mirthful and more cruel, and I think he does it knowingly. The other also applies to the lovers in the net. 'They will not care to lie thus even for a little while longer . . . Soon they will have no desire to sleep together, but the snare and the bond shall hold them.'

The 'delirium passes'.

What is left between them? 'They will have no desire.' The snare and bond will hold them.

III

All in all, this is not a difficult story. I have made comparisons, shown patterns, brought parallels. I could go further. There are many more of them. Yet, as I said in the beginning, the story speaks for itself. It is like an iceberg. A fraction is above the surface. But the mass, the part that is hidden, is essentially the same in content as the part that is visible.

A reader has no need of the additional material. He is able to enjoy 'The Boarding House' on a literal level. It may even be that a consciousness of these voices will impair his enjoyment.

One may also notice that when *Dubliners* appeared, a reader had no way of knowing what was in the letters I have cited. And, before *Ulysses* was written, no one would have thought of looking for a connection between one of these stories and the *Odyssey*. It may be that Joyce, always conscious of posterity, expected that his disciples would in time be able to have the required insights. Yet why would there be disciples? Why should they be so assiduous, so devoted, if they were not captured by the stories on their simple, literal level?

But the voices are there. The letters have been printed. *Ulysses* has been written. They are there. By their presence, they bring a

The Boarding House

weight, a texture. With a pattern of contrast and comparison, they amplify, orchestrate. They ornament; they emphasize.

This is youth: youthful adventure. A hero. A maiden. This is love and sex. This is marriage[1] in Dublin.

---

[1] Joyce's choice of 'Hardwicke Street' may be intended as a veiled allusion to Lord Hardwicke's Act (1751), which regulated marriage contracts. *The Encyclopaedia Britannica* calls it 'a salutary reform of the marriage law which became the basis of all subsequent legislation on the subject'. It is, indeed, probable that Hardwicke Street was named for Lord Hardwicke's grandson, who was a Lieutenant Governor of Ireland.

A Little Cloud

Robert Boyle, S.J.

If we try to reconstruct the imaginative process through which Joyce built 'A Little Cloud', we should concentrate first, I judge, on the scene which ends the story. We see, in a prim room, a rather effeminate man holding his infant son. The baby cries as the father tries to read from a book of poems. Suddenly, trembling with anger, the man bends to the child's face and shouts, 'Stop!'

This 'sudden spiritual manifestation' raises a number of problems. If we saw it without preparation, we might well wonder what motivation could lead to so irrational and even brutal an attack. No normal man, surely, even if irritated by the crying of his baby, would take such measures. Is it an attempt to stifle the child's cries merely, or does it involve some hatred or revenge to explain its savagery? And in this prim and pretty room, and by so neat and prim a man, the act seems especially incongruous.

Joyce builds with great care to this moment of self-revelation. In the course of the four hours or so that the story covers, the spirit of Little Chandler gradually unfolds before our eyes. Considering the structure of this unfolding, I am forced to disagree with a fine critic, James S. Atherton, who says:

'The story is about Little Chandler's failure to live; Joyce begins with the emphasis on Gallaher (the successful journalist whom we meet later in *Ulysses*), but he weaves his two parts together so skillfully that the story remains a unity.'[1]

The story certainly is about Chandler's failure to live. But Joyce begins with the emphasis on Little Chandler, and maintains that

[1] 'The Joyce of *Dubliners*' in *James Joyce Today*, ed. Thomas F. Staley, Bloomington, 1966, p. 50.

emphasis throughout the story. Interesting though Gallaher is, he exists in this story, like all its other elements, to contrast with and to illuminate the spirit of Chandler. We see Gallaher through Chandler's eyes, and it is Chandler's reaction to Gallaher which is central.

The story may profitably be considered in three sections, the first of which reveals the mind of Little Chandler as he anticipates his meeting with Gallaher. The second section covers the meeting of the two men at the bar, and their reactions to one another. The last section deals with Little Chandler's relations with his wife and, especially, with his infant son, and Chandler's reaction to his one decisive act.

The first section of the story reflects the mind, the attitudes, and the language of Thomas Chandler. The opening paragraph indicates that Chandler substitutes language for thought, stock response for genuine emotion.[1] He reveals his own spirit as he thinks in the double language of which Hugh Kenner has so brilliantly written:

'The circumambient language doesn't serve the citizen's thought but directs it. He inherits locutions that were once alive, and shapes his mental processes accordingly . . . Not just the last phrases, but every phrase that passes through Chandler's mind, from "temperament on the point of maturity" to "the Celtic note", is reviewers' jargon; quotation is as close to reality as he gets. Yet it was jargon that had a meaning before the reviewers got hold of it. It contains shreds of meaning still. And Chandler is no contemptible gull; he has really felt some wordless emotion stirring within him, and his melancholy is genuine, and he is seriously meditating a career.'[2]

I doubt the truth of those last two clauses, but the opening paragraph of 'A Little Cloud' illustrates Kenner's remarks about the language of *Dubliners*. It strings together eleven clichés–'seen his

---

[1] Joyce more immediately than most writers manipulates words to his poetic purpose, to give the hearer an experience in sound and meaning analogous to that which the words mirror. Rather than using words merely as a medium for meaning, starting and ending with the meaning, Joyce seems to start with words and end with them so that the meaning is embedded inextricably in these particular words. Like Stephen, he goes to the mystery of reality through words: '. . . and through them he had glimpses of the real world about him.' (*A Portrait*, 64, 62). Joyce's words demand immediate response and constant attention in their careful mirroring of that real world.

[2] *Dublin's Joyce*, London, 1955, and Bloomington, 1956, pp. 8-9.

friend off', 'wished him godspeed', 'had got on', 'travelled air', 'well-cut tweed suit', 'fearless accent', 'few fellows had talents like his', 'unspoiled by such success', 'heart was in the right place', 'deserved to win', 'it was something' – and we perceive at once that Chandler's mind is conventional, limited, insensitive, unperceptive. He is not vigorously alive mentally; he merely shifts one dead phrase into juxtaposition with another. Paralysis has set in, and has almost wiped out any dynamic personal activity in his mind.

His emotional attitudes appear in the images and metaphors he employs. His clerkly work, especially in the light of the 'brilliant figure' he conceives his friend Gallaher to have become, seems tiresome. He is, apparently, a scrivener in the legal line, copying mechanically the embalmed phrases to which the law reduces reality. He sees the depressing figures in the garden outside–untidy nurses, decrepit old men, screaming children–under a romantic haze of 'kindly golden dust'. He feels himself once more becoming a rather bloodless Hamlet figure, seized with what he likes to call 'a gentle melancholy'. He feels that his fortune, unlike Gallaher's, has shut him off from 'life'.

When he was a bachelor, he was free to indulge in at least the beauty and reality of poetry, but since his marriage, he has been too shy to read poems to his wife. But in the lonely solitude of his memory he has found some consolation in repeating the lines he had enjoyed.

His attitude towards children, hinted at in the 'screaming' children in the garden, becomes explicit in the verb and adjective of 'A horde of grimy children populated the street'. They seem to him 'like mice' and 'vermin-like' as he deftly picks his way through them in the growing dark and cold. Their repulsive present activity contrasts with the romantic revelry of 'the old nobility' which in ages past 'had roistered' in these streets. The old English word with its Elizabethan robustness had occurred to Little Chandler in the past, evidently, as did the cavaliers and Swinburnean Atalantas and fancied fears of the following paragraph. Now he is too busy thinking of his meeting with Gallaher to indulge in his habitual romantic daydreaming or nightfearing. Joyce, however, probably enjoyed the irony in Chandler's attitude towards 'roistered', derived from 'rusticus'; the activity admired as noble by Chandler was condemned as barbarously countrified by those to whom the word was once alive.

His admiration for Gallaher rests on a base of Gallaher's free drinking and cadging,[1] and of his wit, a sample of which makes Chandler flush with pride in the remembrance:

'–Half time, now, boys, he used to say light-heartedly. Where's my considering cap?'[2]

He balances Gallaher's cliché with a self-conscious mild oath of his own, '. . . and, damn it . . .'

His association with Gallaher once again exalts him, so that he forgets for the moment his habitual feeling of inferiority. He experiences a novel impulse to revolt against his environment, to escape from it into the freedom and stimulation of cities like London or Paris. He sees and, with a self-conscious 'poetic' effort, sentimentally pities the 'poor stunted houses'.[3] He develops a rather elegant and highly artificial metaphor, which he dreams of embodying in a poem. His idea is indistinct, but the main thing for him is not the poem but the fame and romantic golden haze it would throw around him. Life suddenly seems to spring up within him 'like an infant hope'. Such a feeble and evanescent life, such a little and still 'infant' (the kind of child he wants), can allay the spiritual paralysis a trifle, for, like a knight on quest, 'He stepped onward bravely.'

Light trembles on his mental horizon. He is only thirty-two. He felt grand things within himself, especially melancholy. The melancholy Celtic tone of his poems, embellished by the allusions he would carefully inject, would bring praise from the reviewers.[4] And he would prepare a face to meet those critical faces that he would

---

[1] Noted by Bloom in the 'Hades' chapter of *Ulysses*, speaking of Goulding: 'Waltzing in Stamer street with Ignatius Gallaher on a Sunday morning, the landlady's two hats pinned on his head. Out on the rampage all night.' (109-10, 88).   [2] See Appendix, p. 174.

[3] William York Tindall, in his collection of Joyce pictures, *The Joyce Country*, Philadelphia, 1960, p. 15, has a splendid picture to illustrate what Little Chandler saw from Grattan Bridge.

[4] Mulligan's dealing with 'the Yeats touch' in *Ulysses* (278, 216) inflates the kind of review of which Chandler dreams: 'The most beautiful book that has come out of our country in my time. One thinks of Homer.' And Stephen's sardonic musings about his adolescent dreams concerning his epiphanies (*Ulysses*, 50, 40) echo Chandler's dreams for his poems. The great difference is that Stephen mocks his own immature activity, while Chandler takes his dreams seriously.

venture out to meet by making his name more Irish-looking, 'T. Malone Chandler'.

The second section of the story contrasts Little Chandler's feelings, aspirations, fears, and language with corresponding elements in Ignatius Gallaher. This character interested Joyce, as is evident from his use of him in *Ulysses* and in a reference to him in the *Letters*.[1] He is a journalist, bold, loud, and vulgar, and, even more than Little Chandler, trapped in cliché. When Myles Crawford refers to Gallaher's boast, 'We'll paralyse Europe', he means, I take it, that Gallaher's Irish talent would make Europe stand still with amazed admiration; Joyce meant, I have no doubt, that the dead language and spiritual paralysis of Dublin would be spread to the continent when Gallaher took his moral stagnation and his decayed clichés there. He parrots the jargon of the turn-of-the-century Irish newspaper, 'tasted the joys of connubial bliss', 'may you never die till I shoot you', 'a pleasure deferred'. He uses the cheap and vulgar counters of street-corner toughs, 'a ton better', 'knock about a bit', 'Hot stuff!', 'ready to eat me, man', 'liquor up', 'head in the sack', 'a bit stale'.[2]

Joyce's character is built on Fred Gallaher, a family friend of the Joyces, as Ellmann indicates.[3] Joyce apparently conceived him as embodying traits of Gogarty, since in one of his letters referring to Gogarty's recent and unexpected marriage he repeats the toast Little Chandler promises to Gallaher when he marries.[4]

The reason for Joyce's dubbing him Ignatius can be found, I suspect, in a complex web of association in Joyce's mind. Joyce habitually ties up the artist's vocation with the priest's, and specifically with the Jesuit's. Both Ignatius Loyola, the founder of the Jesuits, who set out from his native land to vivify the world with the cross, and Ignatius Gallaher, who set out to paralyse Europe with the pen,[5] are held up as models to Stephen Dedalus, the first by the

[1] The principal use in *Ulysses* is in the 'Aeolus' chapter. I quote the *Letters* reference below, note 4.

[2] See Appendix, p. 174.

[3] Ellmann, pp. 46–7, n. See Appendix, p. 175.

[4] 'However to be charitable I suppose we had better wish Mr and Mrs Ignatius Gallaher health and long life.' *Letters*, II, p. 148.

[5] When Jaun is choosing his Mass in *Finnegans Wake*, pp. 432–3, he considers the possibilities: 'From the common for ignitious Purpalume to the proper of Francisco Ultramare ...' 'Ignitious' combines, as I read it, the name of Ignatius

88

Jesuits in *A Portrait*, the second by Myles Crawford in *Ulysses*. Furthermore, Joyce conceives of Ignatian behaviour as the exercise of cunning, if we can accept (as I do) the reading of *A Skeleton Key to Finnegans Wake* on this passage:

'He take skiff come first dagrene day overwide tumbler, rough and dark, till when bow of the shower show of the bower with three shirts and a wind, pagoda permettant, crookolevante, the bruce, the coriolano and the ignacio.'[1]

The *Skeleton Key* reads 'the ignacio' as tied up with Stephen's vow to exercise cunning. The low cunning of Gallaher, implicit throughout this story, explicit in the exploit Myles Crawford so admires in *Ulysses*, would help persuade Joyce to name him Ignatius. The names of Jesuit saints, borne by both Joyce and his brother (Aloysius and Stanislaus), were important in the Dublin Joyce knew, and Joyce implies, I believe, that Gallaher has a larger influence on Dublin in general and on Little Chandler in particular than would appear if his name were Fred.

Gallaher patronizes Dublin and Little Chandler, as Chandler soon realizes and resents. He moves to a mild attack, overcoming for a brief moment 'his unfortunate timidity', by suggesting that Gallaher will follow his example and marry. Gallaher reveals, in his own excited resentment of Chandler's challenging claim to this one superiority, that he is not as self-sufficient and balanced as he pretends to be, and he returns and crushes Little Chandler's attack with boasts, loud laughter, and crude insult.

The third section of the story, two or three hours later, shows us Little Chandler's resentment of his trapped situation, his inability to achieve a 'vagrant and triumphant life' like Gallaher's. His humiliation by Gallaher rankles in his soul. He is left to care for the baby while his wife, because of his ineptitude, goes out to buy tea and sugar. He resents his wife, his timidity in buying a blouse for her, her prim complacency in her lack of money and voluptuousness,

---

and his command to his followers to set the world on fire. 'Purpalume' combines the purple prose of the Jesuits, as in the retreat chapter in *A Portrait*, and the plume or pen of the literary artist.

[1] *Finnegans Wake*, p. 228. For the commentary, see *A Skeleton Key to Finnegans Wake* by Joseph Campbell and Henry Morton Robinson, New York, 1944, p. 147, and London, 1947, p. 125. Also see *Letters*, II, p. 134, where Joyce speaks of 'Some cunning Jesuit . . .'

her prim and pretty furniture. Trapped, he might escape if he could write a book like Byron's.

Byron was a romantic rebel, admired by women, a traveller like Gallaher, a fighter like Ignatius. And he wrote poems, like this one which Little Chandler admires because it is so melancholy.[1] It is also, though Little Chandler cannot perceive the fact, a rotten poem, slimy with eighteenth-century clichés, sodden with self-conscious sentiment, puerile in handling of rhythm. The only adequate reason for reprinting it, as Byron himself later realized, is to indicate the difference between this first adolescent product and the more adequate verse its author later wrote.

It is a perfect poem for Little Chandler to admire. First of all, the lack of motion, the darkness, and the narrow cell of death fit with Little Chandler's actual state. The demise of a once-admired woman fits his present feeling towards his wife. Then the poem's deficiencies, to which Chandler is most of all attracted, would be characteristic of his verse could he write any. But he is too paralysed spiritually and artistically to begin to produce even the kind of artistic horror he most admires.

Now the baby intervenes. Its cries force Chandler to break the line of poetry at a significant point, leaving him with the dead clay and without the memory which completes the line, 'such animation beam'd'. Chandler, with all the varied forces of the past few hours working on him and demanding that he focus on the poem, a possible way of escape, resents the child's demands with unaccustomed fierceness. Thus it is that he shouts with anger into the baby's face, and frightens it almost into fits. Here, much more than in his small attack upon Gallaher, where it was said that 'he was aware that he had betrayed himself', he reveals the littleness of his own soul. On his way to Gallaher he ignored the romantic past in quest of a present joy. Here in the face of present and demanding life, which interferes with his pitifully inverted and unreal dream-future, he calls for a stop, and does what he can to destroy the world in which he lives. We can understand with new insight his images about children as vermin. And we see him as an inverted chevalier, re-

---

[1] It was the first poem in *Hours of Idleness: a Series of Poems Original and Translated*, published in 1807. It was titled 'On the Death of a Young Lady' and subtitled 'Cousin to the Author, and very dear to him.' The whole poem is quoted in the Appendix, p. 175.

pulsed in his attack on Gallaher, reduced to attacking the world through his baby, 'Mamma's little lamb of the world!'

What are we to think of his 'remorse'? The word is ambiguous, since it may involve a reform of life, a turning from the thing regretted to something better; or it may merely mean a regret over the past or present state, a pain of loss, like 'agenbite of inwit' in *Ulysses*. Rejected by wife and baby,[1] alone as he has really been throughout his dark and deceived life, Little Chandler in the final paragraph withdraws from the light altogether into a darkness with no romantic golden haze in it, and false tears of remorse start to his eyes. Some consider that the tears portend new life for Chandler, the rain that might come from the little cloud to bring new domestic life. William Powell Jones sees the matter thus:

'He goes home thinking of his frustration, but he sees the responsibilities of home life so sympathetically that he forgets about escape. The frantic crying of his baby and the skilful way his wife handles the situation make him ashamed of having thought of rebellion.'[2]

I cannot agree. Every detail of the story seems to indicate, as I read it, that Chandler's tears, which only start to his eyes, will bring increased irritation rather than new life. These are tears of self-pity, emerging from the darkness of littleness in this selfish little soul, lonely and frustrated. This little Chandler, which means candle-maker, whose light never does shine in the darkness, withdraws from the lamplight into his own little cloud.

Tindall suggests[3] that the title is drawn from I Kings, 18:44, where Elijah produces lifegiving rain from 'a little cloud'. If so, then I see the title as ironic, and the final tears as inadequate to aid in any growth except the increase of sterility in this stunted, timid, inartistic soul.

In this story, then, Joyce reflects in his 'nicely polished looking-glass'[4] the Dublin 'artist', a trapped, ineffectual dreamer. This

---

[1] In the light of Joyce's way with names, it is most likely that the names of Chandler's wife and sister-in-law are deliberately those, not of faithful wives but of famous mothers (Mary's mother and St. Augustine's).

[2] *James Joyce and the Common Reader*, Norman, Oklahoma, 1955, pp. 20–1.

[3] *A Reader's Guide to James Joyce*, London and New York, 1959, pp. 26–7.

[4] *Letters*, I, pp. 63-4: 'It is not my fault that the odour of ashpits and old weeds and offal hangs round my stories. I seriously believe that you will retard the course of civilisation in Ireland by preventing the Irish people from having one good look at themselves in my nicely polished looking-glass.'

Dublin Byron rebels against and attacks only his baby; the language he uses comes largely from a dead and decayed past; the imagery he concocts sentimentally echoes old conventions; he dwells among prim and pretty furniture in a little room off the hall; he cannot emerge from the hell of loneliness in which he is trapped; he is not even able to indulge in violence without shrinking from it in effeminate alarm. He appropriately ends in darkness, able to produce only the start of tears in his inverted and sterile remorse.

Counterparts

Robert Scholes

'Counterparts' offers us, in its title and in its plan, a major clue to the whole structure of *Dubliners*–to the almost musical fabric of themes and variations on the people of Dublin which Joyce has so carefully arranged for us. The title of this story suggests both the harmonious balance of counterpointed musical parts and the anonymous interchangeability of cogs in a great machine. In the story itself, Mr Alleyne bullies the shiftless Farrington and Farrington bullies the hapless Tom. The Farringtons–father and son–are counterparts as unlovely victims. But Farrington and Mr Alleyne are counterparts as abusers of authority. And beyond this story, the brutal Farrington's return to his wifeless home and whining son is the counterpart of Little Chandler's encounter with *his* tiny son in the previous story, 'A Little Cloud'. Similarly, Gallaher in that story is related to Weathers in 'Counterparts', representing an alien London world which challenges and in some sense defeats Dublin (as the Englishman Routh defeats Jimmy Doyle at cards in 'After the Race'). From story to story we can trace strand after strand of such linkage. The 'Gallant' Corley with his slavey's coin in his palm is connected by a thread of counterpointed irony to Lily, the caretaker's bitter daughter (in 'The Dead'), with Gabriel Conroy's clumsily bestowed but well-meant coin clutched in her hands. Gabriel cannot, of course, compensate Lily for a city full of Corleys and Lenehans, and that is part of the irony, but the connection of the coins enriches our perspective on these events and other similar ones with many shades of thought and feeling beyond simple irony. Connections like these, multiplied many times over, are the principal means by which Joyce has blended his separate stories into an imposing portrait of a city and a whole race of people. Not just details, but details alive with echoes and resonances, make these Dubliners vibrate with significance for us.

Farrington himself, waiting for a tram with twopence in his pocket after his evening of frustration, reminds us of the boy in 'Araby', with eightpence in *his* pocket and a fourpenny train ride home ahead of him: both are 'driven and derided' by similar but separate vanities, even as they are frustrated financially. The finances of 'Counter-parts'–so carefully accounted for–remind us of the astonishing role petty cash plays in so many of these stories. The pettiness of Dublin life as Joyce presents it here is in part a response to the pressures of financial distress on a pretentious gentility. The 'Gallant' Lenehan, 'glancing warily up and down the street' lest he should be seen entering a cheap eating house and thereby lose another iota of his remnant of status, is a typical figure in this shabby-genteel society. Even in the upper reaches of Joyce's resolutely middle-class spectrum, Mrs Kearney ('A Mother') grimly struggles for the extra shilling that makes a pound a guinea; and Gabriel Conroy, casting about for a safe subject to cover his sexual embarrassment, mentions to Gretta the surprising return of a pound he had lent Freddy Malins. The question 'And how does he knock it out?' which Mr O'Connor asks Mr Henchy in 'Ivy Day', referring to the disreputable Father Keon, is a great question for many of these Dubliners. M'Coy's stratagem (in 'Grace'), of borrowing (and presumably pawning or selling) valises, echoes the 'Gallant' Lenehan's adroit shifts in sponging. And Weathers's trick of ordering costly Irish and Apollinaris at Farrington's expense makes Farrington think of him as a 'sponge', soaking up the precious six shillings he has obtained by pawning his watch. In story after story, we find ourselves counting shillings and pence. Farrington, insisting on six shillings for his watch instead of the five offered him ('a crown'), is typical of many of these Dubliners in that he has much more trouble 'knocking it out' than modern citizens of affluent societies and welfare states can readily appreciate.

The financial stagnation which contributes to the musty odour Joyce felt he had achieved in *Dubliners* has *its* counterpart in the city's spiritual paralysis. The paralysed priest of 'The Sisters' is a counterpart to the Blessed Margaret Mary Alacoque–the paralytic saint who presides over Eveline Hill's failure of nerve and loss of

faith in her beloved at the North Wall. In 'Counterparts' Farrington's wife seeks at the chapel a consolation which is the counterpart
of that which Farrington seeks in the pub (where a waiter is called a
curate); and little Tom Farrington vainly calls on Mary the Inter-
cessor to save him from the wrath of a father who is definitely not in
heaven. Maria, the virgin of 'Clay', appears on the page following
Tom's invocation, but she is a Peacemaker who cannot even reconcile
her own 'children'; and – though a maiden – she is not blessed but vic-
timized by her celibacy: flustered by an inebriated 'colonel-looking
gentleman', she loses her plumcake; and, confronted with the marriage verse of 'I dreamt that I dwelt', she makes a revealing Freudian
slip by omitting it. But nobody tells her about 'her mistake'. Maria's
spinsterhood, the counterpart of Mr Duffy's purposeful but destructive chastity in the following story ('A Painful Case'), is ironically related to the bad marriage forced upon Bob Doran in 'The
Boarding House' – partly through economic and religious pressure.
(Its badness is confirmed by his reappearing in *Ulysses* as a hopeless
drunkard.) It also reminds us of the other marriages we see, including that of the Farringtons. They are a well-matched couple in
that she 'bullied her husband when he was sober and was bullied
by him when he was drunk'. A puritanical religion of senseless
rigidity insists upon a destructive chastity for these Dubliners, and it
often combines neatly with powerful financial pressures to add to
their worldly torments. The religious and financial motifs of *Dubliners* blend into a symphony of simony in 'Grace', when Father
Purdon encourages commerce between Christ and Mammon, in
the process reducing the spiritual life to the bland mathematics of
book-keeping.

In a letter to his wife, Joyce once explained that he, like other Irish
writers, was trying 'to create a conscience' for his race. This phrase,
which he also gave to his character Stephen Dedalus at the end of *A
Portrait*, has much to do with *Dubliners*. Why, we must ask, should
a people need to have a conscience created for them – especially
a people so conspicuously religious as the Irish? Joyce felt – and
his letters support the evidence of the works themselves – that it was
precisely their religious orthodoxy, combined with other sorts of
'belatedness', that made the Irish so conscienceless. They had turned
over the moral responsibility for their lives to their confessors and

religious leaders. Thus their ability to react sensitively to moral problems, to make ethical discriminations–to use their consciences–had atrophied. In *Dubliners* he offered his countrymen his own counterpart to St Ignatius's *Spiritual Exercises*. The evaluation of motive and responsibility in these stories–the histories of 'painful' cases for the most part–must inevitably lead the reader beyond any easy orthodoxy. These delicately imagined case histories encourage us to exercise our spirits, develop our consciences. They lead us inevitably towards the view that morality is a matter of individual responses to particular situations rather than an automatic invocation of religious or ethical rules of thumb. And though Joyce's own race–the Irish–was first in his mind, he was certainly addressing all of us. Nothing is easier than to slip into the habit of invoking formulae instead of making judgments. New orthodoxies always arise to replace the old. All rebellious prophets tend to become saints in the end–as the history of Freudian ethical thought so clearly shows. But Joyce's painful cases always bring us back to individuality. In entering the world of *Dubliners* we all acknowledge our Irishness. As Martin Cunningham so complacently puts it, 'we're a nice collection of scoundrels, one and all'. But what *we* must see – precisely what Mr Cunningham does not–is that it is our moral complacency that *makes* us scoundrels. Because the spiritual life is an art and not a science, because it is rich and subtle beyond all orthodox formulae, only art can begin to do it justice.

Joyce's art has the necessary delicacy. Not only does Joyce develop a formidable structure of interconnections, making of his separate cases a portrait of a city; he also presents each of these cases with an exquisite control of tone. Inviting us to judge and evaluate, he guides our responses without coercing them; he allows us freedom of response but suggests an order in which some responses are more valuable than others. These stories do justice to the complexity of moral evaluation without denying its possibility. Even Farrington, as crude and simple as any character in the book, is presented with a patient attention to detail that makes him worthy of our interest and prevents us from dismissing his brutality as too banal to require any consideration from us. Joyce's care in such matters is well worth our investigation, for by studying the texture of his work we can begin to appreciate the extent to which his range and power as a writer derive from a delicacy of feeling which manifests itself through his special linguistic gifts. In all his work, Joyce has shown an amazing ability at the fundamental task of poetic or imaginative writing: putting the right words in the right order to do his subject the most justice. And even in a story like 'Counterparts'–a simple episode in the life of a crude man–we can, if we look carefully, discover the sources of Joyce's literary strength.

We can, for example, consider such an apparently trivial thing as the way the narrator of this tale refers to the central character. In the office scenes we learn Farrington's name through its use by Mr Alleyne. But to the narrator–and hence to us–he is just 'The man': 'The man muttered'–'The man entered'–'The man stared'–'The man recognized'–'The man drank'–'The man went'–'The man glanced'–'The man returned'–'The man listened'–'The man got up'–'The man answered'–'The man glanced'. So many simple declarative sentences beginning with 'The man'. Why? What is their effect? The effect–which is worked for us without our being especially aware of how it is managed–is to give us a keen sense of the dull routine of Farrington's existence: of the extent to which he is in his work merely a replaceable cog in a mechanical operation– that sort of counterpart. Calling him 'The man' emphasizes both his dullness and his plain brutal masculinity. And the repetitious sentence pattern drums into our heads the dull round of the man's workaday existence which has certainly helped to brutalize him; just as in the larger pattern of the story the man's bullying of his son shows us the brutalizing process at work upon the coming generation.

After work Farrington becomes more human. He is still sometimes called 'The man' but he is mainly 'He' (as he occasionally was before). In the pawnshop he is reduced to his contractual status–'the con-signor held out for six shillings'–but finally, in the pub, he is given by the narrator for the first time the dignity of being referred to as 'Farrington'. When Nosey Flynn stands 'Farrington a half-one', Farrington has achieved–temporarily–a human individuality which persists until O'Halloran's 'one little smahan more' concludes the evening's festivities. After that we hear his name no more. He is, when we next see him waiting for his tram, not even 'the' but 'a' man: 'A very sullen-faced man stood . . .' And in the final scene we have not 'Farrington' and 'Tom' but 'The man' and 'The little boy', as father and son are reduced by Joyce's distancing conclusion to the general outlines of bully and victim.

In this small matter we can see how Joyce's selection of words and sentence-patterns has conveyed to us the whole rhythm of Farrington's life in the course of presenting a few episodes from it. By such subtle guidance Joyce makes us aware of the quality of Dublin life in all these stories. In the early story 'Araby' the boy hears his uncle come home: 'I heard him talking to himself and heard the hallstand rocking when it had received the weight of his overcoat. I could interpret these signs.' The uncle had been drinking, but we are not told so directly. Like the boy himself we must 'interpret these signs'. This is Joyce's way in story after story. We must interpret for ourselves, but the signs are meaningful, making some interpretations better than others. In the work of interpretation, sifting and weighing details, listening carefully for the various tones of irony and pathos, we develop and refine our consciences.

That this *is* indeed Joyce's way is borne out by some interesting revisions he made in 'Counterparts' between its first completion in July 1905 and the time it appeared in print. Here, for comparison, are the earlier and later versions of a short passage from the pub scene:

1. Farrington said he wouldn't mind having the far one and began to smile at her but when Weathers offered to introduce her he said 'No', he was only chaffing because he knew he had not money enough. She continued to cast bold glances at him and changed the position of her legs often and when she was going out she brushed against his chair and said 'Pardon!' in a Cockney accent.

2. Farrington's eyes wandered at every moment in the direction of one of the young women. There was something striking in her appearance. An immense scarf of peacock-blue muslin was wound round her hat and knotted in a great bow under her chin; and she wore bright yellow gloves, reaching to the elbow. Farrington gazed admiringly at the plump arm which she moved very often and with much grace; and when, after a little time, she answered his gaze he admired still more her large dark brown eyes. The oblique staring expression in them fascinated him. She glanced at him once or twice and, when the party was leaving the room, she brushed against his chair and said *O, pardon!* in a London accent. He watched her leave the room in the hope that she would look back at him, but he was disappointed. (105-6, 95)

These revisions were undertaken in part because a potential publisher felt that there might be objections to the sexual frankness of the passage (though it seems tame enough now). But in working over the passage Joyce himself must have come to agree that the passage was too outspoken–not that it was too licentious but that it was too heavy-handed and obvious, telling the reader too much and not allowing him to infer enough. The narrator of the first version conveys all too clearly his disdain for the 'bold' glances and 'Cockney accent' of the woman. In the second version we are closer to Farrington's own perspective on the scene. We register the impression on him of the woman's graceful arms and fascinating eyes, the alien allure of her 'London accent'. By putting us into closer and more sympathetic touch with Farrington's point of view here, Joyce makes it harder for us to take a merely disdainful attitude towards Farrington. We have enough information to make up our minds about the behaviour of all concerned. We can form our own impression of the 'striking' blue-and-yellow outfit worn by the woman, and we can make the easy inference from 'London' to Cockney. But we must do it ourselves, and we must do it with full awareness of how real and exotic is the appeal of this creature for Farrington. We can see Joyce growing as a writer and as a man in this revision, broadening his range of sympathy and refining his control of irony, moving towards the richness of vision which makes his later work such a rewarding challenge for the thoughtful reader. Joyce invites us to judge Farrington, but he insists that we first understand and feel his situation – that we see the connections between him and his counterparts in all the other stories who feel the appeal of an exotic feminine otherness, including Gabriel Conroy, whose situation is so rooted in Joyce's own biography, and the boy in 'Araby', who is so clearly a counterpart of the young Stephen Dedalus.

Joyce's way, then, as illustrated in this story, is to give us much food for interpretation and put the work of interpretation squarely upon us. He gives us the maximum of conscience-creating labour by inviting us to participate with him in the creative process. To become the ideal reader of *Dubliners* each of us must accept this complicity. Between the mind of the reader and the mind of the artist these stories can flower fully and achieve their richest shape. The opportunity–and the challenge–offered us is that of becoming, in our own small way, Joyce's counterparts.

Clay

Adaline Glasheen

'Clay' is the tenth story of *Dubliners*. It takes place on Hallow Eve, in Dublin, in the early 1900s. The heroine is elderly, runtish, has a witch's profile and no surname. Everyone calls her Maria.

'Maria was a very, very small person indeed but she had a very long nose and a very long chin. She talked a little through her nose, always soothingly: *Yes, my dear*, and *No, my dear*. She was always sent for when the women quarrelled over their tubs and always succeeded in making peace. One day the matron had said to her:

'– Maria, you are a veritable peace-maker!

'And the sub-matron and two of the Board ladies had heard the compliment.' (110, 99)

Maria could not herself write 'Clay'. She is ignorant, unaccomplished. She is aware of herself, but she could not put her knowledge into words. The delicacy, economy and poise of 'Clay' are the work of Joyce, yet 'Clay's' style is like Maria herself. It is a little style, and arch, a style much used by child-minded adults when telling a story to a child–a feebly exclamatory style. And indeed long ago Maria was a children's nurse.

Now Maria is kitchen maid–Cinderella's very own job–at the *Dublin by Lamplight* laundry, a protestant charity, which rescues women from the streets and sets them to reading tracts and washing dirty linen.

Maria is no protestant or fallen. She is Roman Catholic and not fallen. Maria is popular with the staff and with the magdalenes. Everyone has a good word for her, and she is allowed to keep plants in the conservatory. She gives slips to visitors.

Maria, then, is a good little thing. Hardworking, kind and stoic, she is of the same spinster sort as Miss Pynsent in *The Princess Casamassima* and Miss Bates in *Emma*. Maria is good and deserves to get what she wants, and has not gotten, and is not going to get—man, home, children. Maria is not young, but desire has not yet died in her.

Every year on Hallow Eve they eat barmbrack at the *Dublin by Lamplight*. Barmbrack is, as Mr Connolly has pointed out, a divining cake into which a ring is baked. Whoever gets the ring will marry within the year. Though Maria cuts the cake and superintends its serving, she does not get the ring.

'Lizzie Fleming said Maria was sure to get the ring and, though Fleming had said that for so many Hallow Eves, Maria had to laugh and say she didn't want any ring or man either; and when she laughed her grey-green eyes sparkled with disappointed shyness and the tip of her nose nearly met the tip of her chin.' (112, 101)

Men are not known for a willingness to marry a woman without money who has a profile like Mr Punch. The fact is plain to all who know Maria, but Maria is still a woman, cherishing a small, mad hope.

'. . . she took off her working skirt and her house-boots . . . She changed her blouse too and, as she stood before the mirror, she thought of how she used to dress for mass on Sunday morning when she was a young girl; and she looked with quaint affection at the diminutive body which she had so often adorned. In spite of its years she found it a nice tidy little body.' (112-3, 101)

Maria is not going to bed, like Keats's thoughtful Madeline, but is changing to her best clothes because she is going to have an evening out. She is going to spend Hallow Eve with Joe Donnelly and his family. When Joe was a child, Maria nursed him and his brother Alphy; Joe used often to say: 'Mamma is mamma but Maria is my proper mother.' When Maria had charge of Joe and Alphy, they were best of friends, now they are always quarrelling, '. . . but such was life'.

Maria, then, treasures a few poor compliments and three minor, but authentic, talents: making peace, growing plants, engendering affection in children.

Maria goes by tram from Ballsbridge (a southerly part of Dublin) to the Pillar. (The Pillar is Nelson's Pillar—no longer with us—which in 'Clay' and in *Ulysses* Joyce associates with plums and the elderly virgin.) In shops near the Pillar Maria carefully buys penny cakes and a thick slice of plumcake, blushing and smiling when the snippy young lady behind the counter asks 'was it wedding-cake she wanted to buy'.

Then Maria takes another tram to Drumcondra (a northerly part of Dublin). The young men on the tram will not get up and give her a seat, but an elderly 'colonel-looking gentleman' makes room for Maria, chats with her about Hallow Eve and the rain and the good things she is taking to the children. 'Maria agreed with him and favoured him with demure nods and hems.'

'... and when she was getting out at the Canal Bridge she thanked him and bowed, and he bowed to her and raised his hat and smiled agreeably; and while she was going up along the terrace, bending her tiny head under the rain, she thought how easy it was to know a gentleman even when he has a drop taken.' (114, 103)

Things are mildly festive at the Donnellys' house – Joe home, the children in Sunday best, two big girls from next door come to join the fun. Maria gives the penny cakes to the young ones, but the plumcake, meant to be a great treat for Joe and his wife – the plumcake has vanished.

'[Maria] . . . asked all the children had any of them eaten it – by mistake, of course – but the children all said no and looked as if they did not like to eat cakes if they were to be accused of stealing . . . Mrs Donnelly said it was plain that Maria had left it behind her in the tram. Maria, remembering how confused the gentleman . . . had made her, coloured with shame and vexation and disappointment.' (115,103-4)

Maria has lost not only the plumcake, but also her ability to get on with children. She rubs them the wrong way, is not soothing.

The gentleman on the tram has sometimes been accused of having stolen the plumcake, but there is no special reason to think he did, unless indeed he was Corley of 'Two Gallants', disguised. What the missing plumcake shows is that Maria goes all queer in masculine company. Probably it also implies that, as Maria loses her plumcake, so she would lose her virtue, if any man wanted her to lose it. But why would any man?

While the children dance and play games, Maria drinks stout with Joe. A little puffed-up at being a veritable peace-maker, Maria tries to reconcile Joe to his brother Alphy and gets a rough refusal. Most of Maria's tiny talents are tried and found wanting on this Hallow Eve.

The next-door girls arrange a divining game–saucers on a table–ring (marry), water (?), prayer-book (enter a convent). After a while the girls insist Maria play; 'amid laughing and joking' they lead her to the table. To the harmless omens, the young people have added a saucer of wet clay from the garden. Why did they do it? Sheer cussedness? Revenge for having been accused of stealing plum-cake?

Blindfolded, Maria puts her hand into the clay.

'...Mrs Donnelly said something very cross to one of the next-door girls and told her to throw it out at once ... Maria understood that it was wrong that time and so she had to do it over again: and this time she got the prayer-book.' (117, 105)

At the *Dublin by Lamplight*, Maria did not get the ring baked in the barmbrack–no marriage for her. At Donnelly's, Maria's omens are clay and prayer-book, signifying death and a convent before the year is out. To the gods of chance, to the spiteful young, to good Mrs Donnelly, to every discerning eye, Maria's future lies outside the realm of the senses. By every dictate of good taste and good sense, Maria should accede to the secure judgment of the world and kill the nerve that makes her go all wobbly in the company of drop-taken gentlemen on trams.

I think Maria feels the burden of her omens, but she does not say 'Yea' to them. Joe asks her to sing 'one of the old songs', i.e. one of the songs she sang to him when he was a child and she a younger woman. Maria gets up and 'in a tiny quavering voice', sings sensual music.

> *I dreamt that I dwelt in marble halls*
> *With vassals and serfs at my side*
> *And of all who assembled within those walls*
> *That I was the hope and the pride.*
> *I had riches too great to count, could boast*
> *Of a high ancestral name,*
> *But I also dreamt, which pleased me most,*
> *That you loved me still the same.*

And when she has sung it once, incorrigible, she sings it again instead of going on to the second verse, which contains much the same sentiments, but no words so romantic and thrilling as those of the first verse.[1]

Maria loses the second verse of the song much as she lost her plumcake–a man, or the thought of a man, sets her all aflutter.

There is more to be said of Maria's song. It represents Maria's instinctive, scarcely conscious, rejection of the world's judgment of herself. She may not be dead, but they have taken the liberty of burying her in grave or convent. Briefly, vainly she rebels against 'that beast of boredom, common sense'.

Fool that she is, she sings 'I Dreamt that I Dwelt' from Balfe's opera *The Bohemian Girl*. The opera has a Cinderella kind of plot: high-born heroine, Arline (soprano), stolen by gypsies, brought low but destined to mount high, be nobly loved. When Arline sings the aria, she is still a lowly gypsy girl, lowly as Cinderella amid the alien pots and pans. The Cinderella story is the only authentic female myth and as long as it is viable for a woman, she too is viable. The story is still alive for Maria. Briefly, at least, she can imagine herself to be Arline and can be confused by that delicious imagining.

Maria's shabby little rebellion can be compared to Yeats's rebellion when he was an old man.

> *What shall I do with this absurdity–*
> *O heart, O troubled heart–this caricature,*
> *Decrepit age that has been tied to me*
> *As to a dog's tail?*
> *Never had I more*
> *Excited, passionate, fantastical*
> *Imagination, nor an ear and eye*
> *That more expected the impossible–*

Maria has to make do with borrowed rhetoric. Yeats makes his own. But they are talking about the same thing. If the old and ugly feel young and beautiful–what then?

I cannot think that Yeats found an answer to the question any

[1] In all editions of *Dubliners* prior to the new Viking text, edited by Robert Scholes (including Scholes's Cape edition) the first verse of 'I Dreamt' is printed as if it were two verses – break between the fourth and fifth lines. This *seeming* to print two verses of the song makes nonsense of: '. . . and when she came to the second verse she sang again . . .' After I had pointed out the error in his earlier Cape text, Mr Scholes agreed to make the correction in the Viking edition.

more than Maria did. His rebellion against common sense was vastly larger than Maria's and a thousand times better equipped, so that he attained to a gay and Lear-like pitch. Maria's is a cramped little rebellion and she attains nothing higher than a moment of pathos.

Maria's song moves Joe Donnelly to easy tears and another bottle of stout. Maria was Joyce's distant kinswoman and I fancy that, when he heard her sing, he was moved artistically and saw her revealed as a fine small piece of sentimental bravura; in 'The Dead' he repeated the effect–elderly virgin faces death and sings of life: 'Poor Aunt Julia! She, too, would soon be a shade . . . He had caught that haggard look upon her face for a moment when she was singing *Arrayed for the Bridal*.' (254, 222)

Maria is pathetic. Joyce shows her so and leaves her there. 'Clay' does not purge of pity and terror–no story in *Dubliners* does that. 'Clay' leaves you heavy and distended with pity for Maria; 'Clay' leaves you prey to a rising unease, which can swell to terror of the day when you yourself will try to save life within from the bleak judgment of the world. Maria is a silly, but you can count yourself lucky if you manage to mount even so frail a rebellion as hers.

All told, it was not a fun Hallow Eve for Maria. No strong magic came down the chimney and hey presto transformed loathly into lovely lady–Maria the drudge into everyone's hope and pride. Maria will go back across Dublin in the rain to the laundry and find no Porphyrio under her bed. Next morning she will go to Mass. One of her three omens will surely come true–nothing will happen to her, she will die, she will enter a convent. Will gentlemen on trams and love songs confuse her to life's end? Or not? Shall we wish her confused or unconfused? Think carefully before answering the question.

Joyce talked about *Dubliners* being a nicely polished mirror where-in the Irish could see themselves, and–duly horrified–take a first step towards 'spiritual liberation'. Now it is true he was coaxing a publisher, and a writer will say anything to a publisher, but it is also true that *Dubliners* is, as a whole, irradiated with a nagging determin-ation to do good to a lot of people whom Joyce disliked. It is the same spirit that fills *Main Street* and *Winesburg, Ohio* and *John Bull's Other Island*. But when Joyce talked about the spiritual liberation of Ireland, I think he had forgotten 'Clay', an art-for-art's-sake piece of work if there ever was one.

Clay

No specifically Irish paralysis is to blame for the fact that Maria is man-hungry and is not fed. Her plight is supranational, merely human, for as Jane Austen–another spinster–observed: 'A single woman with a very narrow income, must be a ridiculous disagreeable old maid! the proper sport for boys and girls . . .' Maria does not want a spiritually liberated Ireland. She wants Fairyland.

The only lesson to be learned from 'Clay' is that life is unfair and that some of its victims are brave.

A Painful Case

Thomas E. Connolly

When Stanislaus Joyce was almost eighteen years old, he attended a concert at the Rotunda Theatre. At that concert he met a handsome woman of about forty who spoke to him, during the intervals, about the music and about the vocalists. Some time later, Stanislaus met the woman again when she stopped him in the street and inquired about his studies. He never met her again. He did, however, describe these meetings in his diary in which he habitually recorded his experiences, his thoughts on many subjects, his unhappy reactions to his dreary life in Dublin, and, most important, his self-effacing, dog-like devotion to and admiration for his older brother, Jim. Today this diary[1] makes dismal reading, for in it the unhappy Stanislaus laid bare his soul, and the result is unattractive, to say the most charitable thing about it. From time to time, James Joyce would take up his brother's diary to read, and sometimes he would write a scornful remark in it. He expressed his opinion of his brother's soul-probing and confessional unburdening by suggesting that it be titled 'Bile Beans' after a popular laxative cure-all that was offered to the female population of Dublin in large, lurid newspaper advertisements that promised relief from everything from biliousness to bad breath.[2] From this 'unpromising material'[3] James Joyce

[1] *The Dublin Diary of Stanislaus Joyce*, ed. George Harris Healy, London and Ithaca, 1962.

[2] The constant part of the text of these advertisements, which varied in format and in wording from week to week, reads: 'Bile Beans for Biliousness are purely vegetable and are a certain cure for headache, constipation, piles, pimples, blood impurities, bad blood, skin eruptions, liver troubles, bad breath, indigestion, palpitation, loss of appetite, flatulence, dizziness, buzzing in the head, debility, sleeplessness, nervousness, anaemia, and all female ailments.'

[3] Stanislaus Joyce, *My Brother's Keeper*, ed. Richard Ellmann, London and New York, 1958, p. 164-5.

drew the inspiration for the story 'A Painful Case'. It would be a grave mistake, however, to view James Duffy merely as a fictionalized portrait of Stanislaus. He is far more complex than that.

The clues to James Duffy's character and personality are given to the reader first through a description of the room that he occupies in Chapelizod. His room is described as though it were a monk's cell. The lofty walls of the uncarpeted room, we are told, are without pictures or decoration. The furniture is austere: 'a black iron bedstead, an iron washstand, four cane chairs, a clothes-rack, a coal-scuttle, a fender and irons and a square table on which lay a double desk.' The colours that dominate this room are liturgical, black and white. The monastic décor of the room is disrupted by one slash of colour–the scarlet in the extra blanket at the foot of the bed. In this room, the scarlet arrests attention. This colour of passion sets the stage symbolically for the ultimate attraction towards Mrs Sinico that James Duffy experiences, just as the liturgical black and white set the stage for his frantic retreat from her offer of love. The suburb in which Duffy lives echoes this dichotomy. The name 'Chapelizod' is derived from the older form 'Chapel Isod', or 'Yseult's Chapel'. This name continues the combination of the religious theme with the theme of passion. At the beginning of this story of frustrated love, Joyce evokes the archetypal love theme of Tristam and Yseult. Throughout the rest of the story he mingles the two themes.

The number of images in this story that are based on religion or things religious is high. First, we are told that Duffy 'had neither companions nor friends, church nor creed'. Then we learn that he 'lived his spiritual life without any communion with others'. As his friendship with Mrs Sinico grows, 'she became his confessor', and at their final meeting, he thinks of their former meeting place as a 'ruined confessional'. Earlier, before her affectionate gesture frightened Duffy into destroying their relationship, he 'thought that in her eyes he would ascend to an angelical stature'. And finally, in the safety of his cell-like room, when he takes up the account of Mrs Sinico's death, he reads 'it not aloud, but moving his lips as a priest does when he reads the prayers *Secreto*'. This pile-up of religious imagery prepares the reader for a division in Duffy's character.

Next, Joyce turns his descriptive attention to the books in Duffy's library. 'The books on the white wooden shelves were arranged from below upwards according to bulk. A complete Wordsworth stood at one end of the lowest shelf and a copy of the *Maynooth Catechism*, sewn into the cloth cover of a notebook, stood at one end of the top shelf.' Once again, it is important to pay close attention to the details that Joyce gives. The works of Wordsworth are balanced against a slim paper-covered catechism. Though the *Maynooth Catechism* is only a tiny booklet (64 pages in the long version and 32 pages in the short version), it incorporates within its flimsy covers all that is necessary in the way of Christian doctrine, prayers, and lessons to train the Catholic from his First Communion through his Confirmation. It is a detail not to be overlooked. The man who believes himself to be free from church and creed cannot bring himself to discard the catechism of his youth. Not only can he not discard it, but he actually preserves it by sewing it into the cloth cover of a notebook. The description of Duffy's library supports the other hints of a bifurcated personality that Joyce has placed in the opening paragraphs of this story.

Finally, before the beginning of the action of the story proper, Joyce presents two paragraphs in which he describes first the physical appearance of Duffy and then his daily habits of working and eating. (Eating habits will loom large in the later part of the story.) The description of Duffy's face continues the emphasis on a man at odds with himself. The black hair of his head is offset by his tawny moustache and eyebrows. His mouth is unamiable, and his cheekbones give 'his face a harsh character'; but his eyes contradict the impression of his mouth and cheekbones. They give the 'impression of a man ever alert to greet a redeeming instinct in others but often disappointed'.

Here, obviously, rolled into one body, are Shem and Shaun, Jim and Stanny, and it is a fascinating game to trace in the character of James Duffy how much of James Joyce appears and how much of Stanislaus. The sexual frigidity, the abhorrence of drink, and the meticulous scorn of his fellow humans belong to Stanislaus; the socialism, the admiration of *Michael Kramer*, and the attraction to Mrs Sinico belong to James Joyce.

At one point in his diary, Stanislaus Joyce, who normally treats with puritanical harshness his brother's attraction to women, reveals his own human nature at the sight of a pretty, young nurse playing with a dog on a Sunday:

'On the Whitworth Road beyond the deep channel where the railroad runs to my right, a nurse is playing with a black dog in the grounds of the Drumcondra Hospital. I can see she is pretty and young. I would like to be near her, to–. But the wish is impossible. Therefore let it pass . . . Sunday is the worst day of the week–Dull Sunday. And my Sunday, wherein all the dullness of the week is outdone! That nurse! I would like to lie with her in a bed, now, at mid-day, to see her almost stripped in the daylight. Mid-day lechery! But where's the use of this? Though to be sure mid-day lechery is not unusual. The pungent smell of bleached linen being stretched and asperged with cold water and rolled up before ironing excites to cold bright lechery. Such lechery wears an air of health and frankness but loses in sensual intensity. Something in it dissatisfies me. Sunday dinner, Sunday evening yet to be gone through!' (79-80)

Like James Duffy in Mrs Sinico's cottage, Stanislaus Joyce almost comes to life at that point in his diary. Two revealing points that bear on the story, however, are the limitation placed on the desire that surges to the surface: 'almost stripped' and the appetitive substitution 'Sunday dinner'. It is worth noting also that an unusual liturgical term slips into this erotic passage: the linen is 'asperged with cold water'.

By these three devices–colour symbolism, the details of the books on Duffy's shelves, and physical description–Joyce set the stage for the story of a man with a divided character, a bifurcated man who contains within himself the protagonist and the antagonist of the story. A man drawn towards one way of life is anchored in another way of life, and he is incapable of making the transfer. Tragically, his inability to make that transfer destroys a fellow human being, but, even more tragically, it destroys the man himself, and he is a pathetically mute and helpless witness to both acts of destruction.

The texture of this story, which Joyce once called one of the two worst stories in *Dubliners*,[1] is rich indeed, probably because it is one of the most reworked stories in the collection. Professor Magalaner has made an admirable study[2] of this story in which he traces

[1] *Letters*, II, p. 189.
[2] Marvin Magalaner, 'Joyce, Nietzsche, and Hauptmann in James Joyce's "A

the parallels between it and the superman theories of Nietzsche as well as the similarity between the story and Gerhart Hauptmann's play *Michael Kramer*. A point to be noted, however, is that Duffy acquired his books by Nietzsche after he had rejected the love offered by Mrs Sinico. The causes for that rejection were deep within Duffy long before he found external support for them in Nietzsche. That Duffy considers himself to be a superman, there can be no doubt. When Mrs Sinico asks him why he did not write his socialistic thoughts for publication, he answers with crisping scorn: 'For what, he asked her, with careful scorn. To compete with phrasemongers, incapable of thinking consecutively for sixty seconds?' His response to her death is no less Nietzschean: 'Evidently she had been unfit to live, without any strength of purpose, an easy prey to habits, one of the wrecks on which civilisation has been reared.'

Putting aside the Nietzschean view of Duffy, we may view him as the Freudian would, as has Stephen Reid in his study of this story.[1] Reid analyses Duffy from two Freudian vantages. First, he makes a general statement about Duffy: 'In psychoanalytic terminology, James Duffy is clearly a compulsion neurotic.' Then he expounds on both the homosexual and the heterosexual aspects of Duffy's personality. '. . . there is no overt homosexual concern apart from Duffy's single sentence in his notebook. But then we realize that this, too, is part of the picture. Duffy's homosexual impulses are at least as dangerous to him as his heterosexual tendencies. And, with this understanding, we recall Joyce's brief notations of Duffy's avoidance of male company.' Obviously, Reid is concentrating on the significant entry in Duffy's diary (taken by Joyce verbatim from the diary of his brother Stanislaus): 'Love between man and man is impossible because there must not be sexual intercourse and friendship between man and woman is impossible because there must be sexual intercourse.'

Though the term 'compulsion neurotic' is a variant for the more

---

Painful Case"', *PMLA*, 68, March 1953. See also a revision of this article in Marvin Magalaner, *Time of Apprenticeship: The Fiction of Young James Joyce*, London, 1959. Professor Magalaner's analysis of the final paragraphs of the story is especially helpful.

[1] Stephen Reid, ' "The Beast in the Jungle" and "A Painful Case": Two Different Sufferings', *American Imago*, XX, 3, Fall 1963.

familiar term 'compulsive neurotic', they are both acceptable synonyms for Freud's term 'obsessional neurotic'. A psychologist writes:

'As for Reid's citation in Freud of the characteristics associated with a "compulsion neurosis", I presume he referred to a paper by Freud entitled "Character and Anal Eroticism", in which the anal-erotic person is described as being exceptionally orderly, parsimonious, and obstinate. In another of Freud's papers ("The Predisposition to Obsessional Neurosis"), it is stated quite clearly that anal-erotic traits are found in obsessional neurotics (indeed, that they might even predispose an individual to this type of neurosis).'

In view of these comments, how appropriate it is that 'the headline of an advertisement for *Bile Beans* had been pasted on to the first sheet' of Duffy's 'little sheaf of papers held together by a brass pin'.

Finally, Duffy may be examined and classified from another point of view. Early in the story, Joyce invites this approach, which has been carried out in exhaustive detail by Charles D. Wright.[1] In his description of Duffy, Joyce includes this sentence: 'A mediaeval doctor would have called him saturnine.' Wright bases his study on this hint and analyses Duffy and Mrs Sinico as 'humors characters'. 'Mr Duffy and Mrs Sinico,' he writes, 'are both humors characters, melancholy and sanguine, and the story documents in detail "a painful case" of *melancholia*.' The melancholic man is born, of course, under the sign of Saturn. On still another level, then, the pasted advertisement for Bile Beans is relevant, for the melancholic man suffers from an excess of bile, and leading the list of ailments that Bile Beans are guaranteed to cure is biliousness. Wright traces the correspondences between Joyce's description of Duffy and the mediaeval descriptions of the melancholic man. Autumn, he points out, is the season for melancholy, and it is the season in which Duffy breaks with Mrs Sinico as well as the season in which he reads of her death. Music is universally recommended as a remedy for melancholia. The most striking parallel between Duffy and the mediaeval man of melancholy is drawn from Burton's *Anatomy of Melancholy*. From this source we learn that corned beef (the dish Duffy finds unpalatable after reading of Mrs Sinico's death) is expressely condemned by Galen as the worst food for a melancholic man to eat.

[1] Charles D. Wright, 'Melancholy Duffy and Sanguine Sinico: Humors in "A Painful Case"', *James Joyce Quarterly*, III, 3, Spring 1966.

From all these views—the Nietzschean, the Freudian, the melancholic—the reader is left to sort out the significance of 'A Painful Case'.

Whatever the motivating causes that prompted James Duffy to reject Mrs Sinico's offer of love, the major action of the story concerns his responses first to the news of her death and then, more important, to the manner and cause of her death. He initially responds physically; the news 'first attacked his stomach'. Though he is so revolted by the fact that Mrs Sinico had taken to drink that he feels himself degraded and mentally compares her with 'the hobbling wretches whom he had seen carrying cans and bottles to be filled by the barman', his own first impulse is to enter a public house and order a hot punch. The shock of Mrs Sinico's death 'was now attacking his nerves', and 'he called for another punch'. It is curious that Duffy responds in this uncharacteristic way. After the attack on his nerves, which he settles with the very thing that led to Mrs Sinico's death, Duffy's conscience begins to attack, and, as he reviews his life with her, he begins to feel the weight of his guilt. Under the illusion that she is near him in the darkness, he condemns himself: 'Why had he withheld life from her? Why had he sentenced her to death? He felt his moral nature falling to pieces.' He, who had scorned 'an obtuse middle class which entrusted its morality to policemen,' was psychologically and emotionally unable to free himself from those very middle-class codes, and the result was catastrophe. The sight of the two lovers by the Park wall brings this realization home to him, and fills him with despair. With a mixture of gastronomic images, Joyce describes this realization:

'He gnawed the rectitude of his life; he felt that he had been outcast from life's feast. One human being had seemed to love him and he had denied her life and happiness: he had sentenced her to ignominy, a death of shame . . . No one wanted him; he was outcast from life's feast.' (130-1, 117)

After this moral evaluation, Duffy sees the goods train 'like a worm with a fiery head winding through the darkness' along the River Liffey (male and female images, parallel but separate), and he loses all sense of communication with Mrs Sinico. 'He felt that he was alone.'

'A Painful Case' is the last of the individual stories before the final stories that deal with public life. With his homosexual and heterosexual fears, James Duffy appears to be an adult version of the young boy of the first three stories, especially the boy as he is depicted in 'An Encounter', who is so fearful in the presence of the old pæderast. He does, however, carry overtones of the boy as he appears in 'The Sisters', who is at once strongly attracted to Father Flynn and repelled by him. In another way, he is an adult reflection of the boy as he appears in 'Araby', who is disillusioned in his youthful 'puppy love'.

Between the introductory three stories and the terminal three about public life (I exclude 'The Dead' which was added to the original design), the stories in *Dubliners* are arranged in balancing pairs. 'Eveline' and 'After the Race' show male and female views from the state of virginity. 'Two Gallants' and 'The Boarding House' treat of seduction from opposite views in the single life. 'A Little Cloud' and 'Counterparts' deal with frustration of the married male parent. In 'Clay' and 'A Painful Case' Maria is the adult female celibate and James Duffy is the adult male celibate. All the individual stories deal with frustration in the search for some sort of love, be it religious, spiritual, maternal, paternal, or sexual love. From first to last, there is a mounting intensity that culminates, in the most bitter of these stories, 'A Painful Case', in a frustration of love that ends in death.

Ivy Day in the Committee Room

M. J. C. Hodgart

To Stanislaus Joyce (Postcard) MS. Cornell:

1 September 1905   Via S. Nicolò 30, II°, Trieste, Austria
Dear Stannie Thanks for your prompt return of the story with appendage. I send you by this post the eighth story '*Ivy Day in the Committee-Room*' which I hope you will return as promptly . . .

JIM[1]

The story which Stanislaus had returned so promptly was 'A Painful Case', which Joyce had posted about 18 August: 'Ivy Day' was therefore composed or revised during August 1905. About three weeks later he asked Stanislaus: 'Are Aungier St and Wicklow [street] in the Royal Exchange Ward? Can a municipal election take place in October? . . . Kindly answer these questions as quickly as possible'.[2] Stanislaus replied from Dublin on 10 October, 'A Municipal Election *might* take place in October but it is highly improbable. It would be a bye-election (for instance if a councillor or alderman died or resigned) and according to the general rule if it occurred so late would be held over till January. Aungier St is in Royal Exchange Ward.'[3] In the same letter Stanislaus offers the earliest-known criticism of 'Ivy Day': 'accurate, just, and satisfactory. It is original too. I don't think that this which forms so great a part of Dublin, of Irish life has been done before by an artist. To a stranger your differentiation of character would seem nothing less than marvellous. And the poem – the "turn" in this case – is entirely Irish . . .' Joyce was not deterred by the unlikelihood of a municipal election's taking place in October; he had for obvious

---

[1] *Letters*, II, p. 105.   [2] *Ibid.*, p. 109.   [3] *Ibid.*, pp. 114-15.

reasons to place his story on the anniversary of Parnell's death, October 6th.

The long story of his disputes with the publishers over the text of the story can be followed in Ellmann's edition of the *Letters*, volume II; they centred for long on the use of the word 'bloody', e.g. in '–Here's this fellow come to the throne after his bloody owl' mother keeping him out of it till the man was grey . . .' which he altered under pressure to read 'Here's this chap come to the throne after his old mother keeping him out of it till the man was grey . . . ,' but did not change the other occurrence of 'bloody' in *Dubliners*.[1] The famous story of Joyce's appeal to King George V about the passage dealing with Edward VII is described in his letter to the newspapers of 17 August 1911,[2] published by *Sinn Féin* and, with the controversial passage omitted, in the *Northern Whig* (Belfast) in that year. It is worth noting that immediately after Mr Henchy's words quoted above '. . . till the man was grey', Joyce added a sentence for the version as finally published–'He's a man of the world, and he means well by us.' One is not to suppose that this was a conciliatory gesture to the memory of Edward VII; the ribald comments of the Citizen in *Cyclops* indicate the contrary.

From the *Letters* we also learn that 'Ivy Day' was with 'Grace' and 'A Mother' one of the three stories about 'public life';[3] that any Dubliner would 'denounce' it as offensive;[4] and Joyce asks Grant Richards why he does not censure the allusions, not only to the Royal Family, but to the Lord Mayor of Dublin and to the Irish Parliamentary Party. We can therefore take it that Joyce intended this story as a comment on the whole of Dublin political life in the early 1900's. It does not describe an actual election, but is based on the experiences of Stanislaus in 1902. The passage in *My Brother's Keeper* is worth quoting in full:[5]

'Before I entered the accountant's office, my father was temporarily engaged as election agent and canvasser for a candidate in the municipal elections in Dublin, and I as his clerk. Writing to Jim in Paris, I described the committee-room and the people who frequented it just as they appeared in "Ivy Day in the Committee Room". The old caretaker and his family woes, Mr Henchy (a sketch of my father toned down to the surroundings), the other

[1] *Ibid.*, p. 136.   [2] *Ibid.*, pp. 291-3.   [3] *Ibid* , p. 111.
[4] *Ibid.*, p. 134.   [5] London and New York, 1958, pp. 205-6.

canvassers, the unfrocked priest, the wastrel who recites the poem, everything, in fact, except the poem, he got from my letter or from my verbal description when he came home at Christmas. My brother was never in a committee-room in his life. I unwittingly supplied all the material for the story except, as I have said, the poem, which strikes a faint note of pathos and saves the story from being cynical. It is introduced in such a way that, as Padraic Colum observes in his preface to the American edition, despite the hackneyed phrases and the tawdry literary graces, one feels in it a loyalty to the departed chief and a real sorrow.

'Of all the stories in *Dubliners*, "Ivy Day" was the one my brother said he preferred. As for my part in it, I had written and spoken of the committee-room and its canvassers and callers in a mood of sour disgust. It had never entered my mind that there might be material for a story in all that many-faceted squalor. I thought that not only were those Dubliners below literary interest but even below human interest except for hardened philanthropic societies. Still less had it occurred to me that by making a story of it in a spirit of detachment and in a style of "scrupulous meanness", one could liberate one's soul from the contagion of that experience and contemplate it from above with tolerance, even with compassion.'

1902 would seem to be the notional date of the story: King Edward VII's visit to Dublin (July–August 1903) is spoken of as in the future. Parnell has therefore been dead for eleven years, and the background is the slough of despond into which Irish nationalist politics had fallen after the great split. In 1900 Redmond had been elected leader of the re-united parliamentary party which kept its hold on the electorate; but little of interest to Ireland was taking place at Westminster during the long rule of the Tories. There was a general air of defeatism and cynicism over Home Rule; the Dublin electorate was quietist, and the country people were no longer engaged in militant action over land reform. Radical nationalism was kept alive only by a small group of the I.R.B. (Fenians), Gaelic Leaguers, G.A.A. enthusiasts and journalists like Griffith in the *United Irishman* and D. P. Moran in *The Leader*. Hynes belongs to this minority which Mr Henchy calls 'hillsiders and fenians', and of which he uses the contemptuous word 'shoneen' (i.e. little John Bull) which Moran had popularized. Griffith's *Resurrection of Hungary* did not appear till 1904, and his periodical *Sinn Féin* till

1906, in which year the Liberal victory in the general election began the upsurge of serious nationalism that led to 1916. The political implications of the story are clear: almost every Irishman engaged in Dublin politics is a time-server, a sycophant of the British Government and unfaithful to the memory of Parnell. The key passage concerns Edward VII's visit:

'–But look here, John, said Mr O'Connor. Why should we welcome the King of England? Didn't Parnell himself . . .

'– Parnell, said Mr Henchy, is dead. Now, here's the way I look at it . . .' (147-8, 132)

From this superbly ironical indictment no one is spared, even Hynes; he is a hopeless waster, whose political idealism is spilled out in bad verse. Dublin is the centre of political paralysis. In this election to the office of City Councillor, the Conservatives have withdrawn their candidate and are supporting as 'the lesser of two evils' the Nationalist Tierney, and the Conservative canvasser Crofton has been engaged to work for him–that is enough of a comment on Tierney's brand of nationalism. We are not told what party the rival candidate Colgan represents; it is presumably vaguely Labour or Liberal but stands for something fairly innocuous to the Anglo-Irish Ascendancy. The battle is about nothing, and will lead to nothing.

The 'plot' could not be simpler, and observes the 'Aristotelian' unities of time and place. There is a desultory conversation between eight persons, centring on the subjects of politics and parenthood (old Jack and his son, Hynes father and son, Victoria and Edward), and ending with the recital of a ludicrous poem. But it is remarkable how many people are involved during the short 'action'–by the end the stage is crowded with presences. The characters in order of appearance or of being mentioned are as follows:

(a) (present): Old Jack, caretaker; Matthew O'Connor, canvasser; Joe Hynes, journalist; John Henchy, canvasser; 'Father' Keon, occupation unknown; the boy from Tierney's public-house; Crofton, canvasser; Lyons, canvasser.

(b) (absent, living): Richard J. Tierney, publican and Nationalist candidate; old Jack's son; Colgan, bricklayer and rival candidate; King Edward VII; Grimes, voter; Father Burke, nominator; Fanning, sub-sheriff of Dublin; 'a certain little nobleman with a cock-eye'; Kavanagh, publican; Cowley, Alderman; the Lord

Mayor of Dublin; Wilkins, Conservative candidate; Parkes, Atkinson, Ward, voters.

(c) (absent, dead): Larry Hynes (father of Joe Hynes); Jesus Christ; Charles Stewart Parnell; Queen Victoria; Judas.

(d) (mythological or personified): Dublin ('drag the honour of Dublin in the mud'); Erin; the Phoenix.

There are also references to groups of people and institutions, all absent, such as the Christian Brothers, Freemasons, the Corporation of Dublin, the Castle (short for the British Government in Ireland), 'hillsiders and fenians', the Conservative Party, the Nationalist Party, the Roman Catholic Church and its priests (living), Jewish priests (dead). It is hardly necessary to divide the characters into real and fictional or to trace the real originals of the fictional characters in detail. Mr Henchy's conversation, as we have seen, is modelled on that of Joyce's father, John Stanislaus. Crofton (who with Hynes appears again in *Ulysses*) has been identified by Robert M. Adams.[1] There was a real Royal Exchange Ward, and a councillor called Cogan, which is near enough to Colgan, was elected in January 1904. The Lord Mayor whose frugal or plebeian pound of chops is jeered at must have been Timothy Charles Harrington, M.P., who held office from 1901 to 1904: he came of humble origins and had been a wholly loyal Parnellite. (*Finnegans Wake* 447.9: 'Haarington's'.) Fanning is presumably the Long John Fanning of *Ulysses*, modelled on Long John Clancy, the sub-sheriff. But whoever the characters may represent, one thing is obvious: the absent are in general more powerful, both politically in real life and symbolically in the story; and the dead are more powerful than the living. The absent and the dead are summoned up like the ghosts in Homer's Hades (perhaps they come to smell the warm Guinness), but they have the effect of reducing the present and living to the condition of twittering, bat-like shades. The King of the ghosts is Parnell who ends by dominating the whole scene and by extension all Dublin.

This is Joyce's most moving treatment of the theme of Parnell, who haunted him throughout his career. The theme can be followed through the Christmas dinner scene in the *Portrait*, the 'Aeolus', 'Hades', 'Oxen', and 'Eumaeus' chapters of *Ulysses* and in all parts of *Finnegans Wake*. Joyce early came to identify Parnell the

[1] *Surface and Symbol*, Oxford and New York, 1962, pp. 4-6.

Uncrowned King with Christ the King: each was delivered to his enemies by the treachery of his friends. In his article in the *Piccolo della Sera* of 16 May, 1912, 'L'Ombra di Parnell' (the 'shade' again suggests a ghost, as in Yeats's poem) he wrote of Parnell's melancholy conviction 'that in his hour of need, one of the disciples who dipped his hand in the same bowl with him would betray him . . . That he fought to the very end with this desolate certainty in mind is his greatest claim to nobility.' Joyce followed a current notion in identifying Parnell with Moses, the Leader who brought the children of Israel out of Egyptian bondage to within sight of the Promised Land; he develops this trope in 'Aeolus' and in 'The Oxen of the Sun', where Moses is a type of Christ, as in the Liturgy. The trope of the lost leader who will return from the tomb is developed in 'Hades' and further elaborated in *Finnegans Wake*, where Parnell is one of the types of the Phoenix. Joyce's identification of Stephen Dedalus as the Artist with Parnell ('indifferent, paring his fingernails') is well known. One must not suppose that the rich train of association (Parnell–Moses–Christ–Stephen) was in Joyce's mind when he wrote 'Ivy Day'; but the notions of Parnell as ruler ('the only man that could keep that bag of cats in order') and as the Lord betrayed 'to the rabble-rout of fawning priests' are central.

Ellmann notes that, as Joyce hinted, the main device of 'Ivy Day' comes from another story about Christ. Anatole France's 'The Procurator of Judaea' describes Pontius Pilate reminiscing to a friend about the days when he ruled Palestine; there is no mention of Christianity, until at the end the friend asks if he happens to remember anyone called Jesus, to which Pilate replies 'Jesus? Jesus of Nazareth? I cannot call him to mind.' The dead and forgotten Jesus becomes the most important character in the story since without His presence Pilate would himself be forgotten.

The process by which a dead and obscure man takes over the centre of the stage and reduces the living to shadows appears again in 'The Dead', where it is used with even greater subtlety and power. The other literary antecedent of 'Ivy Day' is also a story concerning Christ but less directly. The last sentence – 'Mr Crofton said that it was a very fine piece of writing' – is modelled on the classic anti-climactic last sentence of Flaubert's 'Hérodias' (*Trois Contes*) where the Essenes carry away the severed head of John the Baptist – 'Comme elle était très-lourde, ils la portaient alternativement.' This is the technique which Hemingway imitated and compared to turning down a gas fire very slowly, until it explodes.

Hynes' poem, which according to Ellmann may have been based on one called 'Erin's Heroes' composed by John Stanislaus Joyce and sung by him in 1896, is a masterpiece of bathos. It is a deadly parody of the sentimental patriotic rubbish typical of the Irish popular music of the previous century. Yet it not only conveys Hynes' genuine feelings, to which his audience cannot help responding, but also sums up the basic themes of the story: Christ, traitors, priests, and resurrection 'like the Phœnix from the flames'. Throughout the story the cold and damp of an October evening has been emphasized: the fire of life is almost out. 'Old Jack raked the cinders together'; O'Connor lights his feeble cigarette with an election card; there are only 'a few lumps of coal' for the fire and two candles. Everyone comes in cold, Mr Henchy 'rubbing his hands as if he intended to produce a spark from them'. It is the fire kindled by Parnell in his heyday that has been quenched. '–Musha, God be with them times! said the old man. There was some life in it then.' The talk circles round bad fathers and errant sons: Parnell, unlike Old Jack, Larry Hynes, Victoria or Edward, was the just but stern father who alone could have kept Erin's children in order: '*Down, ye dogs!*' The characters, especially Mr Henchy, present a microcosm of Irish treachery: each politely agrees with the other to his face, only to turn on him with wit and malice behind his back–a notable Irish trait observed by many besides Joyce. But through the absurdities of Hynes' poem there shines, obscurely but unwaveringly, an image of the heroic and lonely men who sacrificed themselves for the Irish cause, to bring about 'the dawning of the day'.

A Mother

David Hayman

'A Mother', the central story in the public life series, is one of the most brutally ironic of Joyce's tales of provincial life. But then the young Irish writer 'self-exiled in upon his ego', living and teaching in Trieste, writing about Dublin and the Dubliners, gave none of his characters his stamp of approval, and the tone throughout *Dubliners* is one of 'scrupulous meanness' despite the lyrical rise that occurs in 'The Dead', a concession to the lingering sweetness of a remembered Dublin. Shortly before he began writing his last tale, the unplanned *coda*, Joyce wrote Stanislaus:

'Sometimes thinking of Ireland it seems to me that I have been unnecessarily harsh. I have reproduced (in *Dubliners* at least) none of the attraction of the city . . . I have not reproduced its ingenuous insularity and its hospitality. The latter "virtue" so far as I can see does not exist elsewhere in Europe. I have not been just to its beauty: for it is more beautiful naturally in my opinion than what I have seen of England, Switzerland, France, Austria or Italy.'[1]

In 'The Dead', then, balancing the ledger without abandoning his ironic stance, he introduced within the genteel if provincial setting what was absent from the grubby occasion at the Antient Concert Rooms, a generous tribute to the Irish arts he himself admired. Thus the background of 'A Mother' finds its foil in the foreground of the later tale, the public performance in the private, just as nationalism and the Irish revival movement which inspire the public concerts are little more than an ominous overtone in 'The Dead'.

If 'Ivy Day in the Committee Room' deals with politics, 'A Mother' with music or public culture, and 'Grace' with public

[1] *Letters*, II, p. 166.

religion or rather popular faith, each of these tales of public life has important sub-themes, echoes items that impinge on the themes of the others. In both 'Ivy Day in the Committee Room' and 'A Mother' human intercourse turns on a preoccupation with payment and, though the emphasis in each is radically different, the implications are not. These characters are self-seekers pretending to a moral position they do not hold, in quest of insignificant and half-earned rewards. On the one hand the rewards are denied and on the other they are bestowed. Paradoxically, it is to the worst parasites that payment is or seems likely to be made, to those facesavers whom Joyce would probably qualify as betrayers. The hired canvassers of a minor politician, the uncultured organizers of a 'cultural event', like the parishioners of a secular faith ('Grace'), are all money-lenders in the temple, symptoms of a degraded culture. Similarly, in each of these stories drink is social currency, and drunkenness is a means of attaining and losing will-power. Joyce uses drinking not so much to condemn vice as to illustrate the lack of purpose and the abdication of responsibility that characterize his male protagonists. It would be possible to understand a character like Hoppy Holohan without knowing that the leech and loafer, the convivial odd-job man, is a Dublin institution, and without recalling that Holohan belongs to the drinking circle of Lenehan and Corley ('Two Gallants'). But without the portrait of the shiftless and indulgent Irishmen who gather around the fire in the bare committee room, we would have only a meagre sense of the values that make his existence possible or of the vacuum that gives birth to a virago like Mrs Kearney. Similarly, in all of these tales there are the ghosts, mock-spiritual emanations that point up hypocrisy and false commitments. There is the ghost of Parnell conjured up in 'paltryattic' verse by Hynes, the political 'spy'. There is the lean apparition of Madame Glynn, the ghost of concerts past. And finally, there is the much abused Holy Ghost bestowing non-alcoholic bliss on the inspirited Mr Kernan. This interweaving of themes and images (and there are many) is deliberate and consistent with Joyce's method elsewhere. Significantly, much that happens in *Dubliners* and 'A Mother' finds echoes in later books, especially in *Ulysses* and *Finnegans Wake*, those repositories for all that impinged on the Joycean consciousness.

Despite its public background, 'A Mother', as Joyce later thought of it and as he doubtless intended, is the clearest exposition of the theme of the dominant female, a type he despised, feared and might have married. Like Emma Bovary, Mrs Kearney (we never learn her first name) has achieved a degree of polish too high for her station. Finding no audience for her acquired tastes and talents (French and music) in the commercial Dublin of her bootmaker husband, she has turned a superficial culture into a whip with which to flog the males who cross her path or into a means of cozening them. Unlike Molly Bloom in *Ulysses* but thoroughly Irish in this, she has sublimated her sex and turned her ivory manners and frustrations against those she feels are her social inferiors. She is a mass of antagonisms. Superficial charm is a mask behind which the supremely competent and ambitious but frustrated woman conceals her *Wille zur Macht*. In 1922, some 17 years after he wrote this story, Joyce, the antifeminist, made a group of notes under its title. He was at the time preparing to write *Finnegans Wake*, and his comments suggest both a biographical basis for the tale and a mocking attitude towards matriarchal and emancipating women: 'gathered to her Mothers: foremothers: W [woman] pays taxes: Vote: . . . *Mrs* and *Mr* Agnes Farrelly . . .'[1]

'A Mother' gives us a portrait of a woman beyond her prime who has reared her unpromising children in her imposing shadow, burying her romantic hopes in their doubtful future, a woman accustomed to commanding her older husband and impelled to work out her frustrations by achieving insignificant goals. Her interest in music and the Irish Revival, even her interest in money (a heavily underlined middle-class trait) are all, Joyce suggests, secondary to a desire to be right, to win out, to control. Music, for this parvenue, is a symbol of the 'good life', the convent culture. Yet, paradoxically, she gives no sign of having any taste. If she is several cuts above the Holohans and Fitzpatricks of the world, her tactlessness and misplaced cult of form make these gentlemen's inadequacies seem like virtues. No less than they, she is an opportunist using culture to advance her social ends.

It may seem strange that this woman, so powerfully bent on social climbing in so limited a sphere, should lose her balance over a few pounds of payment on a contract, but Mrs Kearney, née Devlin,

---

[1] *Scribbledehobble*, ed. Thomas E. Connolly, Evanston, 1961, p. 66. My italics. Slightly corrected. Among these notes is a suggestive reference to Joyce's aunt Josephine: 'Aunt J. salutes when Berty enters.'

is middle-class Dublin to her bootstraps. Beneath the surface, there is always the mental account book which meters the drinks given, the time spent, the tickets bought for those 'who could not be trusted to come otherwise', and even the trimmings bought to spruce up her daughter's gown. For the woman who 'does everything right' without claiming but not without expecting credit for it, the slack behaviour of the impresarios is an intolerable insult, one of many she has had to swallow quietly in the course of her miserable career as wife and mother. The slovenly organizers of cultural disorder are likely targets for her pent-up rage and venom. This is the cause she must have been waiting for since she first felt herself rejected by Dublin's fine young men and out of 'spite' married her dull but docile husband. It is brutally ironic that the cause is so unworthy, that the assault is so ineffectual, that her culture is revealed to be even shallower than that of the Irish barbarians she sneers at.

Joyce seems to have stacked the cards cleverly against her. The concert series, to which her daughter contributes little more than commitment and an artisan's skill, is a failure, but Mrs Kearney cannot afford to blame either her daughter or the people she has helped to organize it. To the extent that it is finally a success, she can expect no praise. The blow to her ego must be countered. She finds her 'objective correlative' in the question of payment and the technicalities of a contractual agreement. Money, the symbol of her existence, becomes the symbol of the outrage she will not endure. It is a matter of principle rather than a matter of taste. In this way she subverts the cause of a 'culture' which has never been deep, substitutes the item gold for the item beauty. Joyce has evolved the perfect metaphor for a sterile passion.

It is the conjunction of the musical event and the ambitious woman, the public and the personal rhythms, that gives this story its dramatic edge and its balance. If the tale of Mrs Kearney hangs on the equation of money and music, the concerts reflect another such attempt to blend oil and water: nationalism and music. This is an affair doomed from the outset to artistic failure. It is, to begin with, overly ambitious in scope. There could not possibly be enough genuinely gifted people available in Dublin to put on a series of four variety concerts. Joyce might have added that there were not enough Dubliners with taste to attend them. We are not told precisely what transpired at the concerts, but it is clear from the reference to Mr

Meade's 'comic turn' and the description of the *artistes* (Joyce makes much of this term) at the Saturday performance that these are over-stuffed affairs designed to provide quantity without quality. The 'Cometty' in charge of arrangements has no taste; its 'best' is not good enough, consisting as it does of amateurs, semi-professionals, and worn-out hacks. The group includes no one of the stature of Molly Bloom or Ben Dollard, those sterling performers whose professional life is part of the texture of *Ulysses*, or even of Bartell D'Arcy, who sings the evocative ballad in 'The Dead'. The best they can do in fact is a dried-up spectre, Mme Glynn, whose echo in *Ulysses*, the singer wife of the Dublin character M'Coy, is a 'Reedy freckled soprano. Cheeseparing nose. Nice enough in its way: for a little ballad. No guts in it.' (92, 76)

In describing the concerts Joyce speaks from experience, though his tone may seem unduly acid. The following quotation from a letter written to his son, Giorgio the aspiring singer, would suggest that 'A Mother' is a post-mortem on Joyce's own dead singing career, a post-mortem written before the remorse had quite worn off: 'Strange coincidence. In my first public concert I too was left in the lurch. The pianist, that is the lady pianist, had gone away right in the middle of the concert. I too sang "Down by the Sally Gardens" and I received exactly 10 dollars or 2 guineas, like you.'[1] Joyce's memory failed him. The concert he describes was his fourth and not his first, though it did contribute at least two details to 'A Mother'. The salary mentioned by Joyce is precisely that promised to Kathleen Kearney. Richard Ellmann's account of the first concert is even more to the point: 'He [Joyce] sang, miserably according to his brother, at a concert given by the St Brigid's Panoramic Choir and Fingall Ladies' Orchestra on the occasion of the Countess Fingall's visit, on Saturday night, May 14[1904].' (Joyce wrote this tale one year later.) The auspices were obviously not the best; perhaps these patriotic ladies were even less prepossessing than the Irish revivalists who put on the fictional series of concerts. According to Ellmann again, just two days after his first concert Joyce appeared as a contender in the Feis Ceoil, a contest he failed to win only because he could not sight read. Disqualified by the rules, he was first awarded an honourable mention, but later, 'when the second place winner was disqualified Joyce received the bronze medal' (which he is said to have thrown

[1] *Letters*, III, p. 340.

into the Liffey river).[1] With what might be considered Flaubertian self-abnegation, or simply monumental scorn, Joyce has included among the performers at the patriotic concert a bronze medal winner, a simple-minded buffoon who could not possibly be more different from Joyce himself.

'Mr Bell, the second tenor, was a fair-haired little man who competed every year for prizes at the Feis Ceoil. On his fourth trial he had been awarded a bronze medal. He was extremely nervous and extremely jealous of other tenors and he covered his nervous jealousy with an ebullient friendliness.' (160, 142-3)

One senses behind the ironic façade more than a little personal spleen, but even so Joyce's choice to present most of these events through the eyes of a mother indicates a remarkable degree of detachment. Like Flaubert, he has chosen to 'describe events from the point of view of a superior joke . . . as God sees them.'[2] It is to this end that he conceived a superbly controlled and versatile or, rather, protean narrator who can shift at will from the voice of Mrs Kearney to a more objective if ironic voice, to a flatly objective voice and finally to an omniscient voice in order to convey the hidden springs of the good woman's character, the reactions of others to her, and the context to which she reacts.

In *Dubliners* in general and perhaps in this story more than most Joyce exploits an essentially lyrical device, permitting the character's voice and reactions to usurp momentarily the narrator's prerogatives. This is of course the technique that illuminates the conclusion of 'The Dead' and the climactic moments of the five chapters of *A Portrait of the Artist as a Young Man*, but here it permits Joyce to light up the character of Mrs Kearney, indirectly to evoke our sympathy as well as our distaste. It is the speed, ease and even grace with which he performs this operation that marks a technical advance over both Flaubert, who seldom understates an effect, and Chekhov, who employs a discreet but emphatic narrator to inform his frequently slight and generally understated situations.

[1] Ellmann, pp. 157-8. See also pp. 173-4 for an account of the fourth concert. In the 'Eumeus' chapter of *Ulysses* Bloom comically connects Stephen with the Fingall Concert: 'Still, supposing he had his father's gift, as he more than suspected, it opened up new vistas in his mind, such as Lady Fingall's Irish industries concert on the preceding Monday, and aristocracy in general.' (*Ulysses*, 742, 663)

[2] Victor Brombert, *The Novels of Flaubert*, Princeton, 1966, p. 22.

From the very start, Joyce mixes fact with illusion, that is, with the subjective vision of his chief persona. Ultimately, it is up to the reader to sort them out and it is to the process of gradual self-enlightenment that we owe our enjoyment of the tangled strands of activity. Even the matter-of-fact tone of the opening paragraph is deceptive, for it includes, among coldly stated facts, what later appears to have been no more than a matter of opinion: that pitiful devil, Hoppy Holohan, we are told, 'walked up and down constantly, stood by the hour at street corners arguing the point and made notes; but in the end it was Mrs Kearney who arranged everything.' The unsuspecting reader is being led into a rhetorical trap. Where do we draw the line between demonstrable fact, or at least credible observation, and the prejudiced viewpoint of an embittered and spiteful lady? We accept at face value the last statement, assuming that a Dublin character like Holohan would be incapable of organizing even a pub crawl. Yet the language is, as we later come to realize, that of Mrs Kearney, and though we never know this for certain, later events point to a considerably smaller part played by that lady. Her ignorance of what, in fact, was happening, her lack of familiarity with the organization that sponsored the events, her inability to judge the performers would indicate that she was outfoxed by the little man and that we in our turn have been deceived by her. Instead of purchasing acquiescence with her whiskey and cookies, she was wasting her substance on a cadger. Hoppy Holohan, like any Dublin drifter worth his salt, can play the dolt while running circles around his victim, even when that person happens to be a hardened ex-romantic 'secret' eater of Turkish Delight. This is not to say that Holohan is an efficient organizer or that he has organized anything at all or even that Mrs Kearney did not contribute her mite to the fiasco. Action is inextricable from motive, but the comedy is inescapable. The woman presented to us in the opening pages is at least partially characterized by her own words, some of which have sinister overtones, undercut though they later are by the facts of her deception. When she plies her willing 'dupe' with whiskey, she sounds a bit like the witch in *Hansel and Gretel*:

'She was invariably friendly and advising – homely, in fact. She pushed the decanter towards him, saying:

'– Now, help yourself, Mr Holohan!

'And while he was helping himself she said:

– Don't be afraid! Don't be afraid of it!' (155, 138)
The point of view here might conceivably be that of Holohan, but
it is most likely that of Mrs Kearney herself. The words conceal a
sly but transparent effort to manipulate an 'obviously' weak man
and the description conveys both overanxiety and a certain coarse-
ness' a lack of style.

Though it is not clear to the reader until the story is well under
way that sharp distinctions among the points of view cannot be made,
the voice of Mrs Kearney soon becomes, if not obtrusive, easier to
recognize. Phrases like 'she never weakened in her religion and was
a good wife to him,' 'she did not like the look of things,' 'began to
express their desire to be entertained,' 'quick stare of contempt'
convey her thoughts with painful directness. Curiously and subtly
they involve us in her attitudes despite our increasing distrust and
even disapproval; for we have no reason to approve of her attitudes.
Joyce had, in the tradition of his French master, made manner fit
matter (or *mater*).

Other expressions are more emphatic and more direct, though
they too are congruent with their more objective context. In a paragraph like the following the indirect narration tells us first about the
character's reactions and then about the event itself:

'When Mrs Kearney arrived with her daughter at the Antient Concert Rooms on Wednesday night she *did not like the look of things*.
A few young men, wearing bright blue badges in their coats, *stood
idle* in the vestibule; none of them wore evening dress. She passed
by with her daughter and a quick glance through the open door of
the hall showed her the cause of the stewards' idleness. *At first she
wondered had she mistaken the hour. No, it was twenty minutes to
eight*'. (156, 139; my italics)

The italicized phrases can fairly definitely be ascribed to Mrs
Kearney. Joyce has deliberately pitched the tone low, so that the
few subjective remarks stand out, but he has also deliberately inter-
mingled objective and subjective elements so that the reader will
absorb them both as part of the texture of experience. A statement
of the time, which would ordinarily suggest no emotional response,
is in this case part of a total and overriding indignation. In the very
next paragraph, the mood, more pronounced this time, takes a
distinctly comic turn with the casual descriptive detail: 'He held a
programme in his hand and, while he was talking to her, he chewed

one end of it into a moist pulp.' Mrs Kearney's acid reaction ('He seemed to bear disappointments lightly') can be interpreted in at least two ways. Either she is aware of his uneasiness before her dragon-like aspect, or she is so self-involved that she fails to recognize the obvious, that she is intruding, that she is quicker to bestow blame than praise, that everybody present is under a strain. As Mrs Kearney's resentment mounts, as the cause for that resentment narrows, and as the 'Cometty' manages to pull its chestnuts from the fire, appearing less and less incompetent though more obviously tasteless, we as readers find ourselves deprived of objects worthy of our sympathy.

In the long final sequence, Mrs Kearney's grievance blooms. The Theatre has filled up for the first time with a satisfactory audience and the more established *artistes* like the first tenor and the baritone have brought 'a breath of opulence among the company'. With nothing but the money on her mind and misplaced pride in her soul, Mrs Kearney strives to have her way, losing ground steadily, despite the ponderous support of a husband whom she herself has rendered ineffectual. As the evening progresses, self-confidence wells up around her, submerging her petty cause in the petty concerns of the others. She is a sour presence, a succubus among the drinking and good cheer. In the end, her cause lost, her mask cracks terribly. She explodes into a common expression before turning into 'an angry stone image.' They had

'treated her scandalously. She had spared neither trouble nor expense and this was how she was repaid.

'They thought they had only a girl to deal with and that, therefore, they could ride roughshod over her . . . They wouldn't have dared to have treated her like that if she had been a man . . .

'– I haven't seen any committee, said Mrs Kearney angrily. My daughter has her contract. She will get four pounds eight into her hand or a foot she won't put on that platform.' (166-7, 148)

It is clearly no longer the daughter who has been offended, but the mother who baldly reveals her envy of men. The shift from indirect discourse, which is obviously almost verbatim, to direct discourse heightens the tension. More important, it exposes Mrs Kearney's pretensions. Her words as she falls into Dublin dialect have a distinctly common ring, a nakedness which is all the more effective in the present context which Joyce has greatly enriched by adding a formidable number of minor characters, calm witnesses whose presence makes her disgrace all the more public and palpable.

In the course of this final sequence, the account of Saturday's concert, the objective voice has become increasingly omniscient, rendering the shallow thoughts of the performers as part of the landscape of the backstage world. Previously, we have perceived the world through the double optics of Mrs Kearney's subjective reactions and the flat factual account of the narrator posing as Mrs Kearney's eyes. Now, though Joyce is careful not to enter the mind of any of the organizers, Mrs Kearney's antagonists, he peppers his text with privileged information, brief analyses of the motivation of the minor *artistes*, as they are affected first by the concert situation and then by Mrs Kearney's behaviour. The sudden but subtle intrusion of an omniscient point of view lightens the text and heightens the drama:

'The first tenor and the baritone and Miss Healy stood together, waiting tranquilly, but Mr Bell's nerves were greatly agitated because he was afraid the audience would think that he had come late.' (164, 146)

Sentences like this one convey a comic but nonetheless real social dimension, a by-product of the battle of wills. They also provide the reader with a fulcrum for his balance and what appears to be a morally tenable position. (We can if we wish sympathize with the innocent.) Joyce resorts to them as infrequently as possible and supplements them with another sort of privileged information, namely the reading of the characters' physical gestures, a reading that differs from Mrs Kearney's in that it does not support her position: 'Mr Kearney continued to stroke his beard and Kathleen looked down, moving the point of her new shoe: it was not her fault.'

Treating gesture as a superior sort of language, Joyce permits his characters' actions to speak more eloquently than their words. Mrs Kearney, who speaks too much and too imperiously, is surrounded by speaking gestures of disapproval and distrust, or worse, of unconcern. To make this point more effectively, Joyce gradually eliminates her point of view in a story that seemed at first to be told very largely in her mirror voice. By the end we no longer overhear her unspoken thoughts though we do hear her heated exchanges with Mr Holohan. To help fill the role of Mrs Kearney's bank of clichés Joyce uses the oily blandness of a journalistic commentator, a voice we may perhaps identify as that of O'Madden Burke: 'Mrs Kearney's conduct was condemned on all hands . . . Miss Healy had kindly consented to play . . .'

In defeat the irate woman has been reduced to the voiceless gestures of frozen rage. Joyce uses biblical imagery to reënforce the shift of field, suggesting through carefully modulated descriptions that Mrs Kearney and her brood have become identified ironically with the family of Lot leaving Sodom. During her last argument with Holohan, 'Her face was inundated with an angry colour and she looked as if she would attack some one with her hands.' Later, faced with general disapproval, 'She stood at the door, haggard with rage, arguing with her husband and daughter, gesticulating with them.' When her cause has finally proved hopeless, 'She stood still for an instant like an angry stone image . . .' and finally on her way out, 'she stopped and glared into Mr Holohan's face.' Then, reversing the biblical tale, she (rather than her husband) herds her family out of Sodom, and in her absence we are permitted for the first time in this tale to read the unspoken sentiments of the self-righteous victor: 'Mr Holohan began to pace up and down the room, in order to cool himself for he felt his skin on fire.' By reversing, even for so short a time, his tactics, bringing us into contact with a figure previously viewed only as an object, Joyce has forced us to modify our emphatically negative judgment of Mrs Kearney. After the stormy exit, we listen to the last word, the sententious statement of O'Madden Burke 'poised upon his umbrella in approval': 'You did the proper thing, Holohan.' If Joyce has turned Mrs Kearney-Lot into a female pharmacos being expelled from the city of the self-righteous, he has simultaneously left his readers without an object for their sympathy, suspended in a void of judgment.

'A Mother' is deceptively simple, so much so that critics generally overlook it, preferring to treat more obviously symbolic stories like 'The Sisters', 'Ivy Day in the Committee Room' or 'The Dead'. In general, it has proved to be a system breaker for the system makers who would force all of *Dubliners* into a symbolic framework. The clever counterpointing of Mrs Kearney and the public event at which she makes herself a public spectacle, the ingenious use of a limited point of view as a means of controlling our sympathies, the ease with which Joyce has suggested his heroine's obscure motivations and surrounded her with a large cast of minor characters, the subtle balance of incident and imagery have gone unnoticed as has the amusingly ironic parallel with the tale of Lot. Despite what might be described as his malicious irony and a lack of detachment from events that after all belonged to his immediate past, Joyce has managed here to dramatize with tact and vigour the dominant themes of *Dubliners*, frustration, boredom and moral paralysis, in terms of frozen movement and fiery rage. The story that begins with Mr Holohan, 'walking up and down Dublin' to no purpose, concludes with the flaming Mr Holohan 'pacing up and down the room, in order to cool himself for he felt his skin on fire.'

Grace

Richard M. Kain

After politics ('Ivy Day in the Committee Room') and art ('A Mother') comes religion, to complete the trilogy of tales devoted to aspects of public life, a trilogy which, in the original arrangement, would have concluded *Dubliners* by balancing the initial trilogy of childhood.

Though it is rich in irony and colourful detail, 'Grace' has seldom received the critical attention it deserves, partly, one suspects, because it is dwarfed by its neighbours, 'Ivy Day' and 'The Dead'. Yet it was originally the finale of *Dubliners*, and it is the only story for which we have assurance of a literary parallel, a method which was to grow increasingly attractive to Joyce. The fall and uncertain redemption of Mr Kernan, both Stuart Gilbert and Joyce's brother Stanislaus have asserted, forms a tripartite parody of the *Divine Comedy*.[1] In its shadowy outline the parallel forms a background against which the human comedy is played. Detailed comment must await our reading of this comedy.

The humour of the story is cumulative, in that the reader's amusement is always directed from the object ridiculed to the norm from which mockery first arose. Mr Kernan's lowly position in drunken stupor at the foot of the lavatory steps is a subject for farce,

---

[1] Stuart Gilbert appears to have been the first, but Stanislaus Joyce is more often cited. Stuart Gilbert, 'James Joyce', in *Writers of Today*, ed. Denys Val Baker, London, 1946, reprinted in *James Joyce: Two Decades of Criticism*, edited by Seon Givens, New York, 1948, p. 461. Stanislaus' first glancing reference occurred in Italian in 1941 but was not translated until 1950, when it appeared as 'James Joyce: A Memoir', *Hudson Review*, II, pp. 485-514. More explicit and extended comment occurs in S. Joyce, 'The Background to *Dubliners*', *The Listener*, 25 March 1954, pp. 526-7.

a literal fall of man. However, the manager of the pub and the customers are soon shown to be less pillars of order than laughably ineffectual humans. The constable is scarcely equal to the occasion. Mrs Kernan, who might be expected to rise above these, does so indeed, but with a difference. Described as 'an active, practical woman' who 'had kept house shrewdly' and had 'healed' her husband 'dutifully whenever he was sick' (i.e. under the influence) she brings to mind the stock comic figure of the shrew. One thinks too of James Thurber's many menacing females. The conspiring friends are not without their own modes of petty deceit (Robert M. Adams has compared them to Job's false comforters[1]). Their would-be profundity regarding the mysteries of the faith and their blunders regarding the Vatican Council make one of the funniest passages in *Dubliners*. All this has been pointing towards 'the retreat business', with the shabby-genteel congregation awaiting Father Purdon. The name suggests 'pardon', but a dubious innuendo is at hand, for Purdon Street, Dublin, was notorious.[2] As these penitents sit self-consciously in their pews they gaze 'formally at the distant speck of red light which was suspended before the high altar'. In this atmosphere the altar light is theatrical (the almost-penitent Kernan had earlier blundered in using the word 'pit' to describe a congregation), yet the light also suggests a distant but perceptible spiritual reality which is the final and most trustworthy standard against which all are found lacking. Everyone but Father Purdon, however, is accorded understanding.

Coming back to those memorable words which the young boy in 'The Sisters' found strangely compelling, 'Grace' is a *gnomon*, an indicator or exposé, of *paralysis* and *simony*, but if it be read merely as another satire of the petty bourgeois much of its effect is lost. Mr Adams wisely observes that both natural and supernatural must be accepted as of worth. For the first, though the companions be 'absurdly wrong' in their confused church history, 'there is a grand resonance to the faith in which they humbly, dumbly dwell'. And only with 'the image of a true and potent church' in mind, Mr Adams concludes, 'can the actual betrayal of the church's ideals, which is reserved for the end of the story, strike with its proper

[1] Robert M. Adams, *James Joyce: Common Sense and Beyond*, New York, 1966, p. 80.
[2] S. Joyce, *The Listener*, 25 March 1954, p. 527.

impact'.[1] Cunningham's description of the Council, Joyce tells us, 'had built up the vast image of the Church in the minds of his hearers', and when Mrs Kernan entered, 'she came into a solemn company'.

Note the appropriateness of the sermon's text: '*For the children of this world are wiser in their generation than the children of light . . .*' These are all 'children of this world'. The unknown 'two gentlemen' who were with Mr Kernan at the pub but who vanished at the moment of his accident and the manager, nervous about the reputation of his establishment, prepare us for the low cunning of the scheming friends with their propaganda for the faith, as this propaganda prepares us for Father Purdon. For Mrs Kernan religion 'was a habit':

'Her beliefs were not extravagant. She believed steadily in the Sacred Heart as the most generally useful of all Catholic devotions and approved of the sacraments. Her faith was bounded by her kitchen but, if she was put to it, she could believe also in the banshee and in the Holy Ghost.' (178, 158)

Above all it is the vulgar Father Purdon who illustrates the wisdom of this world. In a letter to his brother Stanislaus (18 October 1906) Joyce described Father Bernard Vaughan, model for Purdon, as 'the most diverting public figure in England at present'. 'I never see his name', Joyce continued, 'but I expect some enormity.'[2] At the retreat Father Purdon's casuistry was equal to the occasion, and he 'developed the text with resonant assurance'. The rendering of the sermon in indirect discourse subtly underscores the irony, like the final comment of Mr Crofton in 'Ivy Day'. 'It was a text', Father Purdon explained, 'for business men and professional men.' As for himself, 'He told his hearers that he was there that evening for no terrifying, no extravagant purpose; but as a man of the world speaking to his fellow-men.' As 'their spiritual accountant', addressing them 'in a businesslike way', he accommodates the demands of the religious life to his hearers, and to himself.

Father William T. Noon has recently come to the defence of Father Vaughan: 'Though many good-natured jokes were circulated about his flair for dramatic pulpit eloquence, he was on all sides much admired and loved.'[3] He was not Cockney, as Father Conmee

[1] Adams, *op. cit.*, pp. 81-2.   [2] *Letters*, II, p. 182.
[3] William T. Noon, S.J., 'James Joyce: Unfacts, Fiction, and Facts', *PMLA*, LXXVI, 1961, p. 272.

condescendingly remarks in *Ulysses*, but 'celebrated for his Cockney imitations'. Interestingly enough, Father C. C. Martindale's memoir of the celebrated preacher 'quotes the Irish *Freeman's Journal* to the effect that it was once "his wish to be aggregated to the Irish Province of the Society of Jesus and to be stationed at Gardiner Street" – that is, the Jesuit Church of Saint Francis Xavier', the church in 'Grace'. Father Noon finds the character of Father Purdon a gross caricature of his life model, but the recent autobiography of Sir Shane Leslie, *Long Shadows* (1966), offers corroboration to Joyce:

'Vaughan was said to appeal to the old Prince of Wales in the same way as Mrs Langtry – flashy, vulgar, irresistible but both first-class of their kind. Bernard Vaughan had a boxful of music-hall tricks, just as Benson [Father Hugh Benson] had the gestures of a French actor. Vaughan was also an actor, a professional but Benson was an amateur. Vaughan was bombastic at times, a cool and collected sensationalist watching for his chance, and he shouted.'[1]

For the alert reader of Joyce a special delight is the adroit manipulation of tone through language. In 'Grace' false elegance is prominent. Here it is not so much that the style is appropriate to the subject; rather, it becomes the subject. The characters are all 'gentlemen', even the deserting companions at the pub. At the retreat, 'The gentlemen were all well dressed and orderly.' Mr Kernan at first felt a bit self-conscious, but when the moneylenders, a reporter and the down-at-heels O'Carroll were pointed out to him, he 'began to feel more at home'. M'Coy also became aware of the necessary proprieties. His 'comic remarks' going unappreciated, 'he had desisted', for 'Even he was sensible of the decorous atmosphere and even he began to respond to the religious stimulus.'

A useful maxim for readers is that when they think they detect a stylistic gaffe in Joyce they should first suspect intentional mockery. Thus Wyndham Lewis came a cropper in *Time and Western Man* (1927) when he failed to see Joyce's deliberately humorous use of genteel diction. At the beginning of Chapter II in *A Portrait of the Artist as a Young Man* we are told that Stephen's great-uncle Charles smoked such vile-smelling tobacco that Simon Dedalus suggested that he retire to the outhouse. He was amenable to the proposal:

'–Very good, Simon. All serene, Simon, said the old man tranquilly.

[1] Shane Leslie, *Long Shadows*, London, 1966, p. 107.

Anywhere you like. The outhouse will do me nicely: it will be more salubrious.'

In response to Simon's execration of his 'villainous awful tobacco', he replied that it was 'Very cool and mollifying'. Cool and mollifying was his own manner:

'Every morning, therefore, uncle Charles repaired to his outhouse but not before he had creased and brushed scrupulously his back hair and brushed and put on his tall hat. While he smoked the brim of his tall hat and the bowl of his pipe were just visible beyond the jambs of the outhouse door.' (61, 60)

Language is here perfectly in keeping with character and tone. The final glimpse of Uncle Charles brings the episode to the level of cartoon humour. Mr Lewis might have been warned, but he missed all this, and opined solemnly that 'People *repair* to places in works of fiction of the humblest order or in newspaper articles; and *brushed scrupulously*, though harmless certainly, is a conjunction that the fastidious eye would reject.'[1] Precisely. Joyce was unafraid, in fact was delighted to use phrasing from 'fiction of the humblest order or in newspaper articles' (remember 'A Painful Case'), provided, that is, that such clichés served his mimetic purposes. The epiphany, we recall from its definition in *Stephen Hero*, 'meant a sudden spiritual manifestation', but it could occur 'in the vulgarity of speech or of gesture' as well as 'in a memorable phase of the mind itself'. (216, 211) The usual artist is apt to seek the unusual, the memorable. Joyce often bent his attention to subtle revelations of vulgarity.

Uncle Charles wore his hat, happily unaware of his environs, and the gentlemen in 'Grace' do likewise. The hat, and the outhouse, may suggest to us Leopold Bloom; in each case the hat is at once an identifying article of clothing, an ambiguous symbol, and a comic vaudeville prop. In his tumble down the steps Mr Kernan suffered a fall from grace, and so did his hat, battered and rolling away. The hat, like Bloom's cake of soap, has its own Odyssey in this story. It is picked up, then held by a gentleman. It is placed on the injured man's head, and, after its rehabilitation by Mrs Kernan, it too goes to the retreat where it rests on his knees, 'lightly, but firmly' held by its owner. Mrs Kernan's memory of her wedding long ago centred upon the appearance of the bridegroom 'who was dressed

[1] Wyndham Lewis, *Time and Western Man*, London, 1927, p. 126.

smartly in a frock-coat and lavender trousers and carried a silk hat gracefully balanced upon his other arm'. For Joyce the hat plays an important function as he rings changes upon the related associations of the word 'grace', from divine gift to pleasing appearance and manner. Its pertinence to bourgeois respectability is apparent when we are told that as 'a commercial traveller of the old school which believed in the dignity of its calling', Mr Kernan never appeared in the city, 'without a silk hat of some decency and a pair of gaiters'. A man 'could always pass muster', he believed, 'By *grace* of these two articles of clothing' (emphasis mine).

The phrase 'a silk hat of some decency' must be an intentional echo of the popular song which Bloom is later to recall in the funeral carriage as he sees 'a dullgarbed old man' at the curb, silk hat on head:

'Wonder why he was struck off the rolls. Had his house in Hume street . . . Has that silk hat ever since. Relics of old decency. Mourning too. Terrible comedown, poor wretch!'

The chorus of 'The Hat Me Father Wore' goes:

It's old, but it's beautiful, the best was ever seen;
'Twas worn for more than ninety years in that little isle so green.
From my father's great ancestors it descended with galore;
It's a relic of old dacency, is the hat me father wore.

One wonders how Wyndham Lewis would have reacted to the wording 'descended with galore'.

William York Tindall, to whom we are indebted for the emphasis on 'gentlemen' in this story, notes that here as in *Ulysses* 'tea' often occurs in conjunction with 'hat', but that the significance is obscure:

'Content to present, Joyce almost never explains. Tea and hat are unassigned symbols, and we should defer our guesses until we have encountered them again and again in the greater works, where more elaborate contexts may be helpful.'[1]

To follow the associations of these objects through the later books would lead us far afield, to such concepts as creativity, the goddess, the object of a quest, and home. But enough of hats.

False evidence can arouse pathos as well as humour. James Joyce

[1] William York Tindall, *A Reader's Guide to James Joyce*, London and New York, 1959, p. 41.

knew shabby gentility in his father, and in the Dublin around him, but he, 'Sunny Jim' as he was nicknamed, could respond with sympathy, much to the amazement of his Puritanical brother Stanislaus, who reacted constantly with what might be regarded as righteous indignation. Righteous or not, indignation could never inspire such a story as 'Grace'. Its charm is the tone of superiority without disdain which Joyce shares with his readers, a tone carefully controlled by the style of the narrative.

Formal expression gives to this tavern accident a mock-heroic cast. The event is ceremoniously recounted, as befits the self-importance which is assumed by eye-witnesses of no matter how trivial an occurrence. The manager did not simply tell, but 'began to narrate' details of the fall to the immature constable who 'made ready to indite'. Not, however, until after he had 'moved his head slowly to right and left and from the manager to the person on the floor, as if he feared to be the victim of some delusion'. The problem of getting Mr Kernan home was 'debated'. After full discussion of 'the spectacle', 'They agreed that the gentleman must have missed his footing.' In contrast to this elevated language are the muttered comments of the injured and intoxicated Kernan, properly grateful but reluctant to leave and to miss the opportunity of sharing another round. Two days later he had recovered sufficiently to be able to look at his visitors 'a little proudly, with a veteran's pride.' M'Coy, as Coroner's secretary, was 'professionally interested' in the invalid's condition. During the ensuing discussion Mr Fogarty arrived with his half-pint offering of 'special whisky'. 'This new influence', we are told, 'enlivened the conversation'. A second round evokes from the author a lyrical statement: 'The light music of whisky falling into glasses made an agreeable interlude.'

Mr Kernan's befuddled mental processes are analysed with tongue-in-cheek seriousness. We can sympathize with his resistance to the dimly perceived efforts being made to improve his character:

'Mr Kernan was silent. The proposal conveyed very little meaning to his mind but, understanding that some spiritual agencies were about to concern themselves on his behalf, he thought he owed it to his dignity to show a stiff neck'. (184, 163)

His last attempt to save face is his insistence upon not carrying a candle:

'–No, damn it all, said Mr Kernan sensibly, I draw the line there. I'll do the job right enough. I'll do the retreat business and confession, and . . . all that business. But . . . no candles! No, damn it all, I bar the candles!' (194, 171)

A direct quotation, according to Stanislaus Joyce's *Dublin Diary*,[1] from the elder Joyce himself. Another is Kernan's 'I'm not such a bad fellow–' for Stanislaus Joyce noted that Father Vernon, the Jesuit who conducted the retreat, had said of 'Pappie', ' "You're not such a bad fellow after all. Ha! ha! ha! ha!" '. James Joyce's attitude seems to have been similar.

Joyce's affection for his characters extends to their speech. Seldom did he make such extensive use of Dublin idiom, though significant of his final acceptance of common life it underlies the rhythms of *Finnegans Wake*. The inflectional rise of a Dubliner's question cannot be scored in prose, but it can be detected in the young stranger's 'You're all right now?' and in Fogarty's 'Are you sure of that now?' The declarative form of the first question is characteristically Dublin. The reiterative affirmation too: 'That's a fact', 'So he was', 'That is'. And the use of a sentence in place of a clause, in this case the sentence being a question: 'I wonder where did he go to.' These may seem trifles, like the iterative 'at all' and the phrase 'that's a sure five', but they give a flavour unmistakable to one who knows the Dublin turn of speech.

A more pointed irony is the use of the word 'pale' in describing Mr Kernan's less than perfect allegiance to the Catholic church: 'though he had been converted to the Catholic faith at the time of his marriage, he had not been in the pale of the Church for twenty years'. To an Irishman the immediate association of this seemingly innocent word would be with English domination and the hated 'Pale' which from early days surrounded the foreign and later Protestant beach-head in County Dublin. A secondary irony might lie in the association of pallor, for that seems the true colour of faith in Joyce's Dublin.

Joyce tells us that Mr Kernan's social decline – so like the elder Joyce's – 'was mitigated by the fact that certain of those friends who had known him at his highest point of success still esteemed him as a character'. It should be no surprise to readers of this story that

[1] S. Joyce, *The Dublin Diary of Stanislaus Joyce*, ed. George Harris Healey, London and Ithaca, 1962, pp. 77–8.

Joyce himself shared this attitude towards his father, and towards his father's friends. When his father died, Joyce confessed to Miss Weaver: 'I was very fond of him always, being a sinner myself, and even liked his faults.'[1] And to Alfred Bergan:

'You are in this book [*Ulysses*] by name with so many others of Pappie's friends. I remember very well your singing *One of the Family* and *Sister Susie's Playing*. You always made the same mistake in one line of the latter, a mistake prompted by politeness and encouraged by conviviality, for you sang "would make both you and I sick" instead of "would make both me and you sick" '.[1]

Two months later he commented in another letter to Bergan: 'It is strange that after such a long absence I continue to think of all those people, though I have met so many others in different lands.'[2]

In imagination at least Odysseus was looking homeward.

'Grace' shares with 'Ivy Day in the Committee Room' the feeling of being a study for *Ulysses*, which, we recall, was first conceived as a story for *Dubliners*. Both these stories have a strong sense of milieu, that reek of the streets and shabby buildings which permeates *Ulysses*, and both have the same sense of character. Casual links between 'Ivy Day' and 'Grace' can be seen in that two members of the congregation at the retreat, Mr Fanning and Michael Grimes, are referred to in the political discussion of the earlier story. More prominent is the role of Crofton in both stories, as a respectful opponent of Parnell in 'Ivy Day' and in a similar role of dignified opposition as the 'damned decent Orangeman' here.

These two stories contribute more characters to *Ulysses* than any others do, though in this respect 'Grace' is of greater importance. First, Kernan.[3] Throughout the day Bloom has in mind getting tea from him, but characteristically forgets to ask. On the way to the funeral Cunningham ridicules his pompous manner of speech– 'trenchant rendering' and 'retrospective arrangement' are key phrases –and when Mr Power asks about Fogarty Simon Dedalus replies, 'Better ask Tom Kernan', the innuendo being that the pot-washing in 'Grace' was of brief effect. In Glasnevin cemetery he is in character as a sceptical Catholic, expressing a preference for the liturgy of the Church of Ireland. He walks the streets of Dublin later in the

---

[1] *Letters*, I, p. 312. [2] *Letters*, III, pp. 252-3, III, p. 260.
[3] For the appearance of these and other minor characters in *Ulysses*, see Richard M. Kain, *Fabulous Voyager*, Chicago, 1947, pp. 110-11, pp. 252-69.

day ('Wandering Rocks'), happy over the order he has booked, and preens himself before a shop mirror. At the Ormond Hotel ('Sirens') he finds Ben Dollard's singing of 'The Croppy Boy' sufficiently 'trenchant'. Finally Molly Bloom recalls with disgust the episode at the pub: 'that drunken little barrelly man that bit his tongue off falling down the mens WC drunk in some place or other . . .'

Martin Cunningham, who engineers the scheme for getting Kernan to the retreat, plays a subsidiary role of considerable importance in *Ulysses*. He is there characterized by Father John Conmee as a 'Good practical catholic: useful at mission time', and lives up to this description in his efforts to raise a fund for Paddy Dignam's widow. He is also sensitive to the discussion of suicide in the funeral carriage, realizing that Bloom's father had poisoned himself. Bloom had concocted a scheme to get a pass through Cunningham, but that never eventuated. There is no need to follow him through *Ulysses*, nor his companion Jack Power. Both, incidentally, have marital difficulties, Cunningham's wife being an alcoholic, and Power maintaining a barmaid. Together with Crofton, they effect Bloom's escape from the ireful Citizen at Barney Kiernan's. The fact that these characters play so extensive a part in *Ulysses* suggests the possibility that the unwritten story for *Dubliners* may have become transposed into the funeral chapter and the 'Wandering Rocks' episode of the novel.

Long John Fanning also appears briefly, as does M'Coy, again at the old dodge described in 'Grace', namely 'a crusade in search of valises and portmanteaus to enable Mrs M'Coy to fulfil imaginary engagements in the country.' Bloom remembers the valise trick several times during the day of *Ulysses*, having lost one he specially liked, but he also thinks of working M'Coy for a pass. On meeting Bloom in the morning, M'Coy had asked him to put down his name as attending the funeral. Though Bloom is disconcerted at meeting him, he does do this favour, with the result that the *Evening Telegraph* erroneously reports him as attending the service. Thus four of the five penitents, all but Fogarty, are associated with the funeral of Paddy Dignam.

Marvin Magalaner, the first scholar to give an extended analysis of 'Grace', has made the ingenious suggestion that M'Coy 'may well have been an early sketch of the character of Mr Bloom, or Mr Hunter, as the wanderer was originally supposed to have been named.'[1] The parallels are many. Like Bloom an advertising solicitor, his wife also a concert soprano, he shares Bloom's hazy curiosity about things scientific, and, as suggested above but unremarked by Mr Magalaner, he and Bloom are habitual cadgers, M'Coy of valises, Bloom of passes, tea, and many other things. Most important of all is the fact that M'Coy is always the outsider, the man who tries to win friendship but always finds himself snubbed. As Magalaner observes, it is M'Coy who ends up by sitting alone in the Jesuit church, and, ironically, it is M'Coy whom Bloom himself wishes to snub: 'If this hypothesis concerning the origin of Bloom is valid, then, ironically, not even the man who springs from M'Coy wishes to acknowledge him socially.' Magalaner's insight, first published in 1953,[2] was borne out by Richard Ellmann's research for his monumental biography, which revealed that Joyce indeed had one Charles Chance in mind as a model for Leopold Bloom and for his predecessors M'Coy and the Mr Hunter of the unwritten short story 'Ulysses', originally intended for *Dubliners*.[3] Ellmann cites a passage in *Finnegans Wake* which links two of these names: 'Charley Chance (who knows?) so tolloll Mr Hunker.'[4] The *Dublin Diary* of Stanislaus Joyce, which recounts the episode on which 'Grace' was created, identifies Pappie's companions at the retreat as Matthew Kane (Martin Cunningham), Charlie Chance (or M'Coy, as we have seen), and Mr Boyd.

Magalaner makes a further interesting suggestion that Martin Cunningham's resemblance to Shakespeare, reiterated in *Ulysses*, may have been intended to convey a link between Shakespeare and Joyce: 'Thus, by a kind of equation, Cunningham equals Shakespeare equals Stephen-Joyce.' Magalaner notes that Cunningham also shares with Shakespeare and with other prototypes of Joyce an unhappy married life. To his citations of Gabriel Conroy, Little Chandler, and the unloved husband in some of the *Pomes Penyeach* may be added Richard Rowan in *Exiles*, tortured by jealousy and self-distrust. In *Ulysses* Joyce points to numerous parallels between Shakespeare and Stephen, and through Stephen to himself.

[1] Marvin Magalaner, *Time of Apprenticeship: The Fiction of Young James Joyce*, London, 1959, pp. 129-43.
[2] Marvin Magalaner, 'Leopold Bloom before *Ulysses*,' *Modern Language Notes*, LXVIII, 1953, pp. 110-12.
[3] Ellmann, pp. 385-6.   [4] *Finnegans Wake*, p. 65.

It is time to consider the hilarious discussion of Church history by the well-meaning if imperfectly informed council of four who visit the convalescing Kernan. Here we are aided by the efforts of another scholar, Robert M. Adams, who in *Surface and Symbol* uncovered the details of their amusing ignorance.[1] Even without these details we could relish their sage opinions and counsels. Mr Power on Pope Leo XIII: 'I often heard he was one of the most intellectual men in Europe'. Or Fogarty's 'As the poet says: *Great minds are very near to madness.*' The juxtaposition of this last to Joyce's comment that 'Mr Kernan seemed to be troubled in mind' is one of many little ironies in the colloquy. The circular reasoning about infallibility, one suspects, is only a trifle more absurd than sceptics might find the Conciliar deliberations of the subject. And Mr Kernan's uneasy inquiry about papal morality elicits a smile: 'Weren't some of the popes – of course, not our present man, or his predecessor, but some of the old popes – not exactly ... you know ... up to the knocker?' Most readers have seen the absurdity in the pronouncement that 'the Jesuit Order was never once reformed'. 'It never fell away', indeed! Suppressed from 1773 to 1814, it was also expelled many times from France, Spain, and other countries.

To our appreciation of this story Mr Adams supplies not only information but incisive and humorous interpretation. 'There is a cloudy area of facts ill-apprehended, half-recollected, and never understood', he observes, 'where many men, perhaps the majority, spend their intellectual lives'. Joyce delighted in human folly, and even more in the paradoxical wisdom of the foolish:

'Joyce loved to portray a vague, rambling conversation by fuzzy-minded people who know almost nothing of what they are talking about, but who manage, nevertheless, by accumulating small errors, to get pretty close to the main truth.'

The popes do not take mottoes; the source of the phrases is the prediction regarding future popes by the Irish Saint Malachias. 'Lux upon Lux' sounds suspicious, but 'Crux upon Crux' is too good to be true, especially in the context of infallibility. But both are nearly right, Mr Adams finds. Pius IX's was 'Crux de Cruce', and his successor's 'Lumen in Coelo'. Leo did write verse on photography (the appropriateness of the subject to the pope's 'motto' is

[1] Robert M. Adams, *Surface and Symbol*, New York, 1962, pp. 177-81.

not remarked by Mr Adams). The poem is entitled 'Ars Photographia' and rather pompously followed by the date '(An. MDCCC-LXVII)'. Adams supplies the text, and a translation. It was of course not Dowling but the celebrated German professor of theology Johann Joseph Ignaz von Döllinger who opposed the doctrine of papal infallibility. Prominent in political as well as Church affairs, he had written on the Reformation and on Luther. He entered the controversy on infallibility with the *Letters of Janus* (1869) and the convening of a Congress at Nuremburg the following year, but after his excommunication he refused to lead a schism. It would be interesting to investigate the impact his defection had in Ireland and England, but such is beyond the purpose here.

As for the Twentieth Ecumenical Council, it is reported almost accurately by the neighbourhood historians. Mr Fogarty's vague surmise is that 'it was some Italian or American' who held out; it was both. Joyce wrote to his brother (13 November 1906) about looking up the Council in the Biblioteca Vittorio Emanuele in Rome.[1] He reported with deliberate facetiousness that the opposing bishop of Cajazzo was from 'Capuzzo' which in Triestine dialect means 'cabbage'. He continued with the calculation that '*Grace* takes place in 1901 or 2, therefore Kernan at that time 1870 would have been about twenty-five.' He was also checking on Bishop Mac Hale's life and planning to 'rewrite that part of the story'.

Mr Adams has verified one of the points which Joyce was looking up about Mac Hale. He did attend the unveiling of Sir John Gray's statue, as in 'Grace' (Joyce's letter mentioned the Smith O'Brien statue), and, Mr Adams relates, his presence at the ceremony honouring a Protestant was hailed as a sign of religious toleration. Edmund Dwyer Gray was present, but did not speak until the evening: 'Mr Kernan is, thus, right and at the same time wrong–fulfilling thereby, the story's basic image of helpless innocence blundering through a world encrusted with ancient corruption.'

Let us return to the assertion by Stanislaus Joyce that 'Grace' contains a parody of Dante's *Divine Comedy*. Joyce wrote his brother regarding the plan for 'The Last Supper':

'I would like to write *The Last Supper* about Joe MacKernan – ought I? Mother said I was a "mocker". Am I?'[2]

[1] *Letters*, II, pp. 192-3.   [2] *Letters*, II, p. 194.

The tone is scarcely that of a proud Lucifer, arrogant in his blasphemy. Joyce was a mocker, gradually growing more self-assured.

It would be profitless to pursue the parallels in detail, and Joyce may have actually had only the broad resemblance in mind. The filthy floor of the lavatory is an equivalent for Hell, considerably simpler than Dante's complex topography. Resemblances between the fallen Kernan and Milton's fallen angels have been noted.[1] A more biting satire is implicit in the ensuing contrasts with the *Purgatorio* and the *Paradiso*; Purgatory in Kernan's bedroom, with the learned Vergil replaced by the theological bumpkins, and Paradise as the Jesuit church in Gardiner Street presided over by Father Purdon, 'spiritual accountant'. There, amid the blest, pawnbrokers and ward politicians, sits Mr Harford, the moneylender who had conveniently disappeared from Kernan's presence at the time of the accident. In place of Dante's ineffable vision of the Divine Light, 'Grace' concludes with a direct quotation from the priest:

'*Well, I have looked into my accounts. I find this wrong and this wrong. But, with God's grace, I will rectify this and this. I will set right my accounts.*' (198, 174)

In support of the Dantean analogy Mr Magalaner has adduced two corroborative quotations from *Stephen Hero*.[2] In one, Stephen is outraged by 'The ugly artificiality of the lives over which Father Healy was comfortably presiding', and he envisions his companions as 'worthy of some blowing about round the verges of a hell which would be a caricature of Dante's'. Here 'The spirits of the patriotic and religious enthusiasts seemed to him fit to inhabit the fraudulent circles', while 'The spirits of the tame sodalists, unsullied and undeserving, he would petrify amid a ring of Jesuits.' In another episode Stephen comments on the very same Jesuit church in Gardiner Street where the retreat in 'Grace' occurs:

'Everywhere he saw the same flattered affection for the Jesuits who are in the habit of attaching to their order the souls of thousands of the insecurely respectable middle-class by offering them a refined asylum, an interested, a considerate confessional, a particular

---

[1] Marvin Magalaner, *Time of Apprenticeship: The Fiction of Young James Joyce*, London, 1959, p. 131.

[2] *Ibid.*, pp. 100–1. The citations are from *Stephen Hero*, 163–4, 158–9, and 124–5, 119–20).

amiableness of manners which their spiritual adventures in no way
entitled them to.'

The heavy underscoring, characteristic of *Stephen Hero*, contrasts
with the urbane irony of 'Grace'. In *A Portrait of the Artist as a
Young Man* too Joyce is willing to let a direct quotation prove his
point. Echoing M'Coy's remark about the Jesuits, 'They're the
boyos have influence,' Mr Dedalus says:

'let him stick to the jesuits in God's name since he began with them.
They'll be of service to him in after years. Those are the fellows
that can get you a position.' (73, 71)

Apropos of Dante, Hugh Kenner has made the interesting suggestion that the 'quincunx' of penitents may derive from the group-
ing of the courageous in Dante's fifth heaven.[1] The chiastic emblem,
a cross within a circle, symbolizes in its perfection of form the
mystery of redemption. To quote from the translation of Laurence
Binyon:

> *So in the depth of Mars were clustered those*
> *Full beams to make the venerated sign*
> *Which quadrants, joined within a round, compose.*
>
> *Par.* xiv, 100-102.

If Joyce parodied Dante, it was, as later with Homer, as much an
act of fealty as of mockery. He had prided himself on his knowledge
of Italian in his University College days, and championed Dante
alone with Ibsen and Bruno, a trinity of exiles and recreants. Later
he was to win the alliterative sobriquet of 'Dublin's Dante' from
John Eglinton, Oliver Gogarty, and others. His friend Padraic
Colum had noted his 'Dantesque face and steely blue eyes', and
Joyce certainly gloried in the resemblances.[2] For all the resemblances,
the mask of the stern Florentine did not fit perfectly the laughing
Dubliner, who was often more mimic than moralist. Hence inter-
preters frequently find themselves less forgiving of the characters
than the author. The contrast with *Stephen Hero* indicates both a
gain in technical control and a mellowing of attitude.

It was in Rome during the winter of 1906-7 that Joyce first

[1] Hugh Kenner, *Dublin's Joyce*, London, 1955, and Bloomington, 1956, pp.
61-2.
[2] Estella Ruth Taylor, *The Modern Irish Writers, Cross Currents of Criticism*,
Lawrence, Kansas, 1954, p. 67.

expressed nostalgia for the Dublin he had left two years before. 'Rome reminds me of a man who lives by exhibiting to travellers his grandmother's corpse,' he wrote his brother. The tedium of his bank job, the heat of the late summer, the bureaucracy of officialdom all made him long for 'a seaside place in England or Ireland'. A completely bourgeois dream, with 'rashers and eggs in the morning, the English variety of sunshine, a beefsteak with boiled potatoes and onions, a pier at night or a beach and cigarettes'. In this mood he wrote the letter in which he said he feared that he had not reproduced in *Dubliners* the attraction of the city, and yet, he concluded, such reflections were useless, for, were he to rewrite, he would 'find again what you call the Holy Ghost sitting in the ink-bottle and the perverse devil of my literary conscience sitting on the hump of my pen'.[1] But 'The Dead' was to come, touches were to be added to 'A Painful Case' and 'Grace', and Joyce even thought of beginning 'Ulysses' and 'The Last Supper'.

It is odd that only one of the letters cited here was included in the first selection of correspondence edited by Stuart Gilbert; apart from Frank Budgen's book, and some observations by the present author, little was known of Joyce's warmth for Dublin and Dubliners until the publication of Richard Ellmann's biography in 1959, and the equally imposing two additional volumes of letters six years later. Meanwhile it seemed an almost official line to consider Joyce's rejection of his native city as utterly uncompromising. Even so, when Julian B. Kaye wrote of 'Grace' in 1957 he sensed that though the Church is 'thoroughly corrupted by simony' the conversation of the friends is 'amusing rather than painful because of its brilliant social comedy.'[2] The already cited study by Marvin Magalaner is another exception to the prevailing moralistic reading. A further brilliant insight into Joyce's comic vision by Magalaner must be mentioned, that is, 'A parallel between the Dublin police force and the Dublin priesthood', twin pillars of social and of spiritual security with crowded pub and immense constable paralleled by crowded church and heavy priest.

The moral vision is present, even though it be interrupted by muffled laughter. J. Mitchell Morse, a theological student outside

[1] *Letters*, II, pp. 165, 157, 166.
[2] Julian B. Kaye, 'Simony, the Three Simons, and Joycean Myth', *A James Joyce Miscellany*, New York, 1957, p. 23.

the tradition of scholasticism, has portrayed Joyce as *The Sympathetic Alien* (1959), taking the title for his study of Joyce and Catholicism from a passage in *Stephen Hero* which reflects the same priest-police syndrome:

'As Stephen looked at the big square block of masonry looming before them through the faint daylight, he re-entered again in thought the seminarist life which he had led for so many years, to the understanding of the narrow activities of which he could now in a moment bring the spirit of an acute sympathetic alien. He recognised at once the martial mind of the Irish Church in the style of this ecclesiastical barracks.'[1]

Professor Morse applies Aquinas to his diagnosis of the sins exemplified in 'Grace', finding Kernan effeminate in his drinking, presumptuous in his worldliness, as are his companions, and, together with them and Father Purdon, 'spiritually pusillanimous' in seeking 'a "fine, jolly fellow" of a priest, who will spare them the depths and the heights of religious experience'.[2] The travesty of religion in general, and of Grace in particular, is so pervasive in this story that it can hardly be over-emphasized. Here Grace is equated with Works, and that on the most petty level of accounting. One scarcely needs Dante to understand this, but the grand structure of the *Divine Comedy* provides a measure of this pettiness.

Joyce's relish of pertinent detail yields so many rewards to the scrupulous reader that it may seem ungracious to consider some critical findings less convincing than others. In the reading of *Dubliners* as a 'First Flight to Ithaca'[3] Richard Levin and Charles Shattuck adduced numerous correspondences, many of which would undoubtedly have pleased, even if they might have surprised, the author. To see the first three stories, like the opening chapters of *Ulysses*, as a Telemachia, a search of the son for the father, is brilliant. Eveline makes a plausible Calypso, but could well be a Nausicaa (but Nausicaa is the servant girl in 'Two Gallants'). There is an appropriateness to the close as a homecoming, especially as it applies to the 'reunion with Penelope' in 'The Dead'. 'Grace' as an aspect of this homecoming seems less relevant: Kernan as Odysseus, a

---

[1] Pp. 72-3, 77.

[2] J. Mitchell Morse, *The Sympathetic Alien*, New York, 1959, pp. 108-9.

[3] *Accent*, IV, 1944, pp. 75-99, reprinted in *James Joyce; Two Decades of Criticism*, ed. Seon Givens, New York, 1948, pp. 75-99.

commercial traveller, filthy as the Homeric hero was in beggar's garb, may be acceptable, and Mrs Kernan as Penelope. The authors admit that after the early part of the story 'analogues of action . . . are not many'.

Brewster Ghiselin has also contributed brilliant insights in reading *Dubliners* as 'one essential history, that of the soul of a people which has confused and weakened its relation to the source of spiritual life and cannot restore it'.[1] Contrasting images of enclosure and of escape seem pertinent, but specific labels for colours, and the assignment of meanings to east and west, or to articles of clothing may be less so. In this reading 'Grace' belongs to a group of stories emblemizing 'the subversion of the cardinal virtues of justice ["Ivy Day"], temperance ["A Mother"], and prudence ["Grace"].' It would seem that the applications of temperance and prudence could just as easily be interchanged.

When one surveys specific applications of the symbolic method to slight details it becomes apparent that Joyce's mode of analogy can lead to almost uncontrolled associations on the part of the imaginative reader. It may be a significant fact that both Power and Cunningham work for the English, Power in the Constabulary Office and Cunningham at the Castle, but are we to make much of the reference to Power's *ulster*?[2] To see in that familiar article of clothing 'the colour of orient light' as one commentator has it,[3] and on the other hand to find a sinister pairing of *power* and *cunning* in the two men's names[4] is to reach a point where interpretations cancel one another. Recently a critic has found Mars in the red altar light and in Cunningham's first name, *Mar*tin.[5] Is Kernan's refusal of the candle (as we have seen, taken from life) a rejection of illumination?[6] Following Mars once more, the fact that the circle of the courageous in the *Paradiso* is the midpoint of the heavenly pattern has been seen as evidence of mediocrity.[7] The midpoint of the *Inferno*, we learn, is that of the flatterers, and Kernan makes a

[1] Brewster Ghiselin, 'The Unity of Joyce's *Dubliners*', *Accent*, XVI, 1956, pp. 75-88, 196-213.

[2] Stanley L. Jedynak, 'Epiphany and Dantean Correspondence in Joyce's *Dubliners*: A Study in Structure', Ph.D. Dissertation, (1962), Xerox copy, p. 190.

[3] Ghiselin, *op. cit.*, p. 207.

[4] Carl Niemeyer, ' "Grace" and Joyce's Method of Parody', *College English*, XXVII, December 1965, pp. 196-201.

[5] *Idem.*   [6] Ghiselin, *loc. cit.*   [7] Niemeyer, *op. cit.*

living by his tongue as a tea-taster! But is he in any way a flatterer?
Elsewhere we are told that the penitents kneel 'in the polysymbolic
attitude of drunken paralysis, of shrinking from the breath of the
soul's orient' (presumably of the altar light).[1] More appealing is the
suggestion that the candles indicate a parallel to the Feast of Candle-
mas, and of the Epiphany season (and Joyce's birthday), and
provide a corresponding chord to the candles at the house of the
dead Father Flynn, with which *Dubliners* opens.[2]

Another ingenious reading (forgetting Fogarty) finds the Trinity
in the story, Mr Power as God, the cunning Cunningham as Christ
(through the concept of the Logos), and 'the real M'Coy' as the
Holy Ghost. It is 'only to lead us astray' that Cunningham is older
than Power, but soon we are brought back by Cunningham's
resemblance to Shakespeare and Power's use of the Shakespearean
cliché, 'all's well'. And, by the way, Cunningham's first name surely
suggests Martin Luther, as his setting up house for his drunk and
disorderly wife no less than six times seems to parallel some 'six
episodes in Church history', the Church being the bride of Christ
(no matter how drunk and disorderly!). After this last *aperçu* the
author well concludes that 'It is indeed hard to decide where our
speculation should stop.'[3]

Regardless of where we choose to stop, 'Grace' remains basically
a story which combines moral intent, satiric humour, and mocking
parody, and yet in essence is a nostalgic evocation of the shabby
and needy but appealing Dublin life from which Joyce exiled himself and which he was already yearning to revisit, at least through the
vicarious method of recreating it through language.

[1] Ghiselin, *loc. cit.*
[2] Florence L. Walzl, 'The Liturgy of the Epiphany Season and the Epiphanies
of Joyce', *PMLA*, LXXX, September 1965, p. 449.
[3] Joseph E. Baker, 'The Trinity in Joyce's "Grace"', *James Joyce Quarterly*,
II, 1965, pp. 299-303.

The Dead

Bernard Benstock

The motif of death is solidly established in the coda story of *Dubliners*, not only with Joyce's succinct title, but with the various rhetorical devices embedded in the terse opening sentence: 'Lily, the caretaker's daughter, was literally run off her feet'. Lily's tag-name, that of the funereal flower, serves as a symbol of death—as well as an ironic allusion to purity; the connotation of 'caretaker' is mere innuendo, since we later realize that he is custodian of the estate, rather than of a cemetery, but by then the effect is unalterable, and the smell of the graveyard is in our nostrils; and the hyperbolic figure of speech ('run off her feet'), which although figurative, is offered to the reader to be accepted 'literally'. Yet this early impregnation of death symbolism is soon belied ostensibly by the pleasant Christmas setting, the musical entertainment, the sentimental speech, the 'gourmeterring and gourmandising'—the *élan vital* of the story's surface. The hostesses bubble and flitter about; Freddy is hilariously drunk; Browne lecherously enthusiastic; and Gabriel Conroy himself seems the embodiment of contented self-importance. The dead appear far removed from the celebration of the Nativity.

The dead are very much in evidence, however, and death hovers over the feast at all times, emerging triumphant by the end. Three levels of these dead become apparent upon close examination: the deceased, the moribund, and the living-dead, the composition of the last group expanding with the progression of the story. Four of the 'dear departed' remembered and acknowledged during the course of the evening's activities are: Gabriel's mother, whose 'last long illness' he recalls in conjunction with her 'sullen opposition to his marriage' to Gretta ('Some slighting phrases she had used still rankled in his memory; she had once spoken of Gretta as being country cute'); the two Patrick Morkans, 'brother Pat' (Mary Jane's father, whose death terminated the residence of his sisters in Stoney Batter) and 'the old gentleman' (whose horse Johnny had circled the equestrian statue of King Billy in mesmerized paralysis); and finally Michael Furey, whose spectre takes possession of the tale in a way comparable to Parnell's domination of 'Ivy Day in the Committee Room'. These in turn are represented by the array of opera singers conjured up during dinner (dating back to the Parkinson remembered only by the oldest participant) and even by the snow-covered statue of Daniel O'Connell.

Those obviously close to death are the three old women, Aunts Kate and Julia and Mrs Malins. Aunt Julia, whose 'flaccid' face is grey with 'darker shadows', has the 'appearance of a woman who did not know where she was or where she was going'. Aunt Kate, whose face is healthier, nonetheless has a face 'like a shrivelled red apple', and is 'too feeble to go about much'. And Mrs Malins is 'a stout feeble old woman with white hair'. There is enough evidence, therefore, from Joyce's capsule descriptions of them, for the reader to realize, even before Gabriel's awareness late in 'The Dead' of the imminence of Julia's death, that these old and sickly women are re-minders of the final gasp of life. Their totems are the monks of Mount Melleray who sleep in their coffins 'to remind them of their last end'.

But old age is not the only requisite for inclusion among the moribund, as Gabriel also comes to realize, since time brings all men towards death: 'One by one they were all becoming shades. Better pass boldly into that other world, in the full glory of some passion, than fade and wither dismally with age.' Such passionate glory is denied to the living-dead, those who remain alive, but fail to live: the disillusioned, the self-destructive, the blighted and wasted lives. It is with these that 'The Dead' is most concerned. First there is the servant girl Lily, just out of school and already cynically world-weary, presumably because of a prematurely un-pleasant experience with a man. The mature and proper Gabriel is actually shocked at her assertion that 'The men that is now is only all palaver and what they can get out of you.' And although we are informed that 'she got on well with her three mistresses', a change is mirrored in Kate's recent disappointment: 'I'm sure I don't know what has come over her lately. She's not the girl she was at all.' (No longer a girl, Lily has been initiated into womanhood, and it is not difficult to speculate about what has come over her lately.) Less serious reminders are seen in Mary Jane, in her thirties and unmarried, who plays 'Academy pieces' on the piano that no one listens to; Freddy Malins and Browne have their obvious vices; and Bartell D'Arcy, the much-praised tenor, is hoarse and consequently rather grouchy. Most important of course is the revelation that Gretta has been living a dead life in contrast to the remembered and cherished romance of her youth, a revelation that destroys the bubble of her husband's unreal existence, permanently deflating the self-assurance of his artificially bolstered world.

Even for those who are quick to perceive 'the skull beneath the skin' of most of the characters in 'The Dead', the Conroys at first seem to be a healthy contrast. Had there not been so much dynamic spontaneity associated with them, as they came in out of the snow much anticipated and warmly welcomed (Gabriel scrapes the snow from his shoes 'vigorously'; his clothes emit 'a cold fragrant air from out-of-doors', while Gretta goes upstairs with the aunts 'laughing'), perhaps we might have been more suspicious of their poses. Surely the opening conversation contains enough indications that all is not sound as Gretta goodnaturedly belittles her husband's prissy solicitousness: Gabriel is worried that his country wife will catch cold and has therefore engaged a hotel room in order to avoid the return home to Monkstown late at night. Gretta ridicules his insistence upon goloshes ('Guttapercha things', she calls them), and doubles her scorn by crediting his faith in them as both conformity and affectation: 'Gabriel says everyone wears them on the continent.' (Buck Mulligan sneers at Stephen: 'O, damn you and your Paris fads.') Worse still, Gretta compounds his faults almost maliciously: 'He's really an awful bother', she reports to his aunts in his presence, 'what with green shades for Tom's eyes at night and making him do the dumb-bells, and forcing Eva to eat the stirabout.' And finally she boasts of her successful rebellion against him, that on this particular evening she refused to wear her goloshes despite the snowfall. None of this, however, is as heavy as it might sound, extrapolated this way, but an important barometer of Gretta's effect on her husband's sensitivity can be seen from the changes in his attitudes as she babbles away: at first he answers his wife's glance with 'admiring and happy eyes', and we learn that 'Gabriel's solicitude was a standing joke' with the aunts, but the goloshes prove too sore a point ('Gabriel knitted his brows . . . as if he were slightly angered') –it takes Aunt Kate's tact to change the subject. Beneath Gretta's delightful banter, therefore, can be seen a slight but significant rift in the marital lute, and Mrs Conroy's objection to Gretta's country-cuteness might suggest a disparity in social levels, that her good looks have netted her the climb through marriage into the solid middle class.

Class distinctions are not irrelevant in 'The Dead'. Next to the son of a merchant-prince butcher in 'After the Race', this last story gives the reader a glimpse into the best of the middle class in a volume whose range includes every aspect of the bourgeois spectrum. (There is almost a touch of Dickens when Gabriel thinks, 'People, perhaps, were standing in the snow on the quay outside, gazing up at the lighted windows and listening to the waltz music.') But economic decline, an important factor in the depiction of the Dedalus family of *A Portrait*, is in evidence. The Morkans delight in living well, as attested by their annual fête and their general insistence upon the best in food ('diamond-bone sirloins, three-shilling tea and the best bottled stout'), but their rented floors in the 'dark gaunt house' on Usher's Island represent a significant change from the house in Stoney Batter, and their zeal in preventing Mary Jane's pupils, who came from 'the better-class families on the Kingstown and Dalkey line', from being discomfited by Freddy's drunkenness mirrors an attitude of social subservience. (Mary Jane personally serves as waitress for these pupils, offering them the best.) The three Graces have been reduced to selling their talents while nurturing their bourgeois assumptions that music is not a commodity like corn, the source of income for the Mr Fulham who owns their house and conducts his business on its ground floor. Ironically they also disclose their middle-class snobbery by insisting that the 'old gentleman,' their father, had owned a starch mill rather than a glue factory. ('Well, glue or starch', says Gabriel democratically, his intellectual snobbery sparing him the necessity of the snobbery of his class.) From affluent mill-owner to shabby-genteel music teachers indicates another Joycean irony. Yet the cause of the financial decline is somewhat unusual: it can be assumed that with the death of Brother Pat no male was left to run the business–the masculine line had run out, leaving only women. Pat's only child (at least from internal evidence) is also female, and only one of his sisters married, producing two sons, neither one of whom she groomed to soil his hands boiling starch (or glue). The priest and the teacher fulfil the family ideals of their class, rising above its mercantile level, but leaving the Morkans unable to reproduce themselves.

The musical Morkans by their very talent contain the seed of their own destruction. We have seen from 'A Mother' the extent to which music is a dead end in Dublin; in a nation which considers vocal music its principal art form, a concert like the four-part series scheduled for the Antient Concert Rooms proves to be an acid test of the state of art in general in Ireland's capital city. Joyce has indicated that the trio of stories preceding 'The Dead' ('Ivy Day', 'A Mother', 'Grace') concentrate on the public life of the city, isolating politics, art, and religion as areas of focus. The closing story summarizes this concentration as well as all themes inherent throughout *Dubliners*. Joe Hynes' sincere if ineptly expressed Parnellism is in healthy contrast to the betrayers in the Committee Room, but emerges as the narrow nationalism of Molly Ivors in 'The Dead'. The cash-register Catholicism of Father Purdon's sermon for businessmen is reduced to Gabriel's Christmas gratuity to Lily and Freddy Malins' Christmas-card shop, while the vestiges of Tom Kernan's Protestant objection to candles can be seen in Protestant Browne at the Morkans' party, in front of whom the Catholics fear that they are 'giving scandal'. In general, religion as a dead end is personified by the Mount Melleray monks in their coffins. And the failure of the concert series is prolonged in the reaction to Mary Jane's piano piece (which bores Gabriel and causes the four topers to slink away to the bar, returning only at the conclusion to offer the 'most vigorous clapping'). D'Arcy's singing of 'The Lass of Aughrim' receives a better response, although he himself proves irritable because of his hoarseness, but Gretta's reaction of intent rapture is due to personal nostalgia rather than critical appreciation. In contrast to these 'failures', however, we seem to have the very substantial success of Aunt Julia's rendition of 'Arrayed for the Bridal', where even the performer is moved by the applause which 'sounded so genuine'. Apparently a genuine response is a rarity (which in itself should make us suspicious), but

Julia's triumph is tinged with irony. She is many years past her prime and in the process of being replaced by boy sopranos in the choir at Adam and Eve's Church. When Gabriel, who 'applauded loudly with all the others' at the time, later realizes that he 'caught that haggard look upon her face for a moment when she was singing', the full horror of the phenomenon should become apparent. 'Arrayed for the Bridal', as incongruous a selection for the ageing spinster as 'I dreamt that I Dwelt' was for Maria in 'Clay', is Julia's beautifully executed Swan Song.

Joyce's comment that he might have been 'unnecessarily harsh' in his treatment of the moral state of affairs in Ireland (made after the first fourteen stories had gone to the publisher but before he wrote 'The Dead'), may indicate that the added *novella* was in some way intended to offset the effect of the preceding epiphanies. Yet in dozens of small correspondences 'The Dead' serves as a summation of the entire volume. The religion-art-politics of the immediate predecessors re-emerge here, while the breakdown of family relationships in those stories is paralleled as well: father-son in 'Ivy Day' (not only the caretaker, Jack, and his profligate son, but the contrast established by Henchy between Joe Hynes and his father), mother-daughter in 'A Mother' (although Mrs Kearney's domination of her husband is also important), and husband-wife in 'Grace' (if Tom Kernan is a cross for his wife to bear, Martin Cunningham has one in his wife). The destruction of the superficial harmony of the married Conroys is well anticipated. And what are we to assume about the names Tom and Eva for the Conroy children? In 'Counterparts' Farrington has a son named Tom whom he beats for letting the fire go out; by way of contrast, Gabriel, a very different sort of father, is concerned about his son's muscles and eyes. (Two adults are also named Thomas: Chandler and Kernan.) And is Eva to remind us of Eveline Hill? Her relationship with her father has certainly soured. With the reference to Kathleen Kearney in 'The Dead' we find the first instance in which a previous *Dubliners* character is mentioned, the beginning of a process that Joyce went on to exploit fully, as both Kathleen and Gretta figure in Molly Bloom's thoughts.

The key words of the first paragraph of the first *Dubliners* tale (paralysis, simony, gnomon) are significant in varying degrees for every one of the fifteen stories, and reach their culmination in 'The

Dead'. The whole process of the Morkans' soirée is a repeated one, so that even the reader (for whom this is a fresh experience) soon begins to feel an aura of *déjà vu* (Gretta caught cold after last year's party; Freddy can be expected to be drunk again). The participants themselves know the formula, as can be seen when Bartell D'Arcy, apparently a newcomer, at first refuses to allow his glass to be filled, until 'one of his neighbours nudged him and whispered something at him'–the ceremonial toast is next on the programme. The 'never-to-be-forgotten Johnny' is almost a parody of the theme of paralysis, and one might suspect that Daniel O'Connell, frozen in stone and covered with snow, is still another. The instances of simony are perhaps subtler, but the birth that took place in a manger among shepherds is being celebrated here in high style with the best of everything among the comfortable bourgeoisie, while irresponsible Freddy pays his debts after having cashed in on the Nativity by way of a Christmas-card shop. Even Gabriel is guilty of simony when, unnerved by his awkward conversation with Lily, he gives her a coin in order to cover his embarrassment, and when her attempt at refusal further discomfits him, he credits Christ as a precedent: '–Christmas-time! Christmas-time! said Gabriel, almost trotting to the stairs and waving his hand to her in deprecation.' The Euclidian gnomon, however, has drawn little notice from commentators on *Dubliners*, yet that 'part of the parallelogram that remains after a similar parallelogram is taken away from one of its corners' (*O.E.D.*) offers us an insight into the author's technique in the book, where we come to understand the nature of the substance from its shadow. Father Flynn is that removed entity in 'The Sisters', Mrs Hill in 'Eveline', Mrs Sinico in 'A Painful Case' (where the title itself is gnomonic), Parnell in 'Ivy Day in the Committee Room', and of course Michael Furey in 'The Dead'.

Gabriel Conroy no more escapes the paralysis of Dublin than any of the other protagonists in the *Dubliners* stories, as he himself comes to realize during his epiphany. As a man of sensitivity and intelligence he becomes aware of the significance of the epiphany (like the boy in 'Araby', James Duffy, and to a lesser extent Little Chandler). Material comfort, intellectual superiority, an important position, and distinction as a reviewer of books do not qualify him for exemption from the paralytic situation: he remains rooted in the centre of the paralysis. At best he is a part-time tourist, not an exile;

a continental cyclist, not a 'hawklike man'. He has reached the prime of life without realizing that he too shares the fate of the Freddy Malinses and Mr Brownes. Yet the surface evidence is at first deceptive (both to Gabriel and to the reader who takes him at face value): we can assume that his choice of a Browning quotation indicates a real degree of poetic appreciation (unlike Chandler's choice of Byron juvenilia), and that his book reviews reach an audience (unlike Duffy's sequestered translations and aphorisms). But the literary critic and the teacher of literature are poor substitutes for the creative artist, and vacationing on the continent is but temporary escape. Gabriel's self-deception is as serious as Chandler's or Duffy's and has been far more successful until the night of the Morkan party. We never learn whether Gabriel's epiphany redeems him, but we can assume that he is redeemable: he is a younger man than James Duffy and has not cut off all avenues of contact with the outside world; unlike the adolescent in 'Araby' he is mature enough to cope with 'anguish and anger'; and he is spared the intellectual pretention of Chandler, while country-cute Gretta will obviously prove less of a burden than the pretty-faced Annie.

The road leading to the destruction of Gabriel Conroy's inflated ego is lined with a succession of women. It is highly ironic that his lack of sophistication in handling women should prove to be so instrumental, but the entire evening is progressively ruined for him by this shortcoming. Perception in dealing with the masculine world is apparent in Gabriel: he is elected to apprehend Freddy upon his arrival and gauge the severity of his drunkenness; he can determine from the 'indelicate clacking of the men's heels and the shuffling of their soles' that he 'would only make himself ridiculous by quoting poetry to them which they could not understand'—and he makes his adjustment accordingly.

With men his defences are air-tight, but with women he is virtually defenceless. He starts out on the wrong foot with Lily and never recovers his equilibrium, yet the barely literate girl should hardly be a match for the articulate and worldly Gabriel. Only a year or so out of school, she is hardened into a cynicism which shreds the mature man's naiveté with a single ungrammatical sentence. He has no sooner recovered from this encounter than his own wife has her chance at him (goloshes, dumb-bells, eye shades, stirabout), the worshipful aunts, whose 'favourite nephew' he is, joining in ('Gabriel's solicitude was a standing joke with them'). Then Molly Ivors all but demolishes him. Her intentions seem to be honourable: 'I have a crow to pluck with you,' she says, and we can conclude that she proposes a friendly discussion over a difference of attitude; there is also her invitation that he join her and her faction on their Irish vacation. Her tone is one of flirtatious teasing and it is again a commentary on Gabriel's lack of *savoir faire* that his hackles rise (Richard Rowan certainly handled Beatrice Justice with far greater dexterity). She is coy, she is cute, she squeezes his hand, whispers in his ear, smiles at him and gazes into his eyes, but Gabriel is made nervous, he blushes, he tries to 'cover his agitation' and finally concludes that she 'had tried to make him ridiculous before people, heckling him and staring at him with her rabbit's eyes'. Even when he has recovered, the best he can do is gallantly offer to see her home when she attempts to leave. There is no doubt that Gabriel is ripe for Gretta's final twist of the knife. His self-delusion of strength is merely a matter of his never really having been challenged before.

Gabriel yearns for escape. He may appear to be at home in the warm surroundings of the social event, in his 'well-filled shirt-front', but he dreams of being outside, detached from it all. (Mr Duffy 'lived at a little distance from his body', but Gabriel lives too close to his.) Waves of anxiety mix with moments of self-confidence, as each discomfort is compensated for by a minor triumph. Lily's disdain for his paternalism at first causes him to doubt the success of his speech ('He would fail with them just as he had failed with the girl in the pantry. He had taken up a wrong tone. His whole speech was a mistake from first to last, an utter failure.'). But the gush of affection from his aunts dispels his pessimism, and he responds to Gretta's opening volley of teasing with 'happy eyes'. When Gretta goes too far, he again sinks into a sombre mood, 'as if he were slightly angered', until his successful shepherding of the tipsy Freddy restores him. So the pattern develops: he finds Mary Jane's piano piece too academic but lacks the courage to be as impolite as the four young men in the doorway and walk out on it; instead he remains, although his eyes are 'irritated by the floor, which glittered with beeswax', and only a picture of his mother soothes him (until he remembers her contempt for Gretta). It is Miss Ivors' turn then to chip away at his ego, and his contemplation of revenge, public insult incorporated into his after-dinner talk, assuages him, so that he can afford to be magnanimous in offering to escort the 'retreating' Molly. But before his plan has taken form in his mind, Gabriel leans against the window and realizes: 'How cool it must be outside! How pleasant it would be to walk out alone, first along by the river and then through the park! The snow would be lying on the branches of the trees and forming a bright cap on the top of the Wellington Monument. How much more pleasant it would be there than at the supper-table!' Thoughts of the masculine symbol, erect in the park, revive him, but his dreams are in vain of course; he is committed to the supper-table and the party for the entire evening. It is Molly Ivors who escapes, whose 'retreat' further accentuates her victory over paralysed Gabriel. Yet he misinterprets the significance of her departure, and gains ebullient self-assurance: 'Here I am, Aunt Kate! cried Gabriel, with sudden animation, ready to carve a flock of geese, if necessary.'

With malicious Molly gone, the hero begins to achieve a series of victories to offset her effects. Carving the goose is the first: 'He felt quite at ease now for he was an expert carver and liked nothing better than to find himself at the head of a well-laden table.' He misses the irony that he who had yearned for the cold outdoors should content himself with his indoor employment, 'for he had found the carving hot work'. When he is about to begin his speech, he again thinks of the outdoors ('The air was pure there')–his fingers are 'trembling' and he smiles 'nervously'. But the speech is a grand success, minus the bothersome quotation from Browning, for which he has substituted the dig at Miss Ivors. (That she has escaped his barb does not seem to faze Gabriel, who seems quite satisfied with his hollow victory.) This second irony is followed by still a third: in the hallway before departure, Gabriel scores his finest social coup of the evening in recalling the anecdote of his grandfather and the never-to-be-forgotten Johnny, apparently for the edification of Mrs Browne of all people. The worm has turned: it is Gabriel's turn to tease and taunt now, as he tells his version of the story about the 'old gentleman', against the gentle protests of Aunt Kate. 'A very pompous old gentleman', Gabriel labels him, unaware of his own pomposity, his 'well-filled shirt-front'. In fine humour he finally emerges into the cold night air, achieving his escape at last, and contemplating enjoyment of the spoils of victory.

The contrast between cold and warmth hints at a symbolic understructure in 'The Dead' that is far more complex than in any of the previous stories. Critics have suggested that the fire in 'Ivy Day', for example, indicates a scene in Hell (giving neither warmth nor light), when in actuality Joyce employs fire often in *Dubliners* with just this sort of emphasis: as fire in 'Counterparts', 'Clay', and 'Ivy Day in the Committee Room'; as artificial lights and candles in 'The Sisters', 'Araby', 'The Boarding House', 'Two Gallants', and 'Grace'; sunsets and sunrises in 'Eveline', 'After the Race', 'A Little Cloud', and 'A Painful Case'. In summation 'The Dead' contains all of these. The artificial lighting in the Gresham Hotel is out ('The porter pointed to the tap of the electric-light and began a muttered apology'), but Gabriel rejects the candle ('I bar the candles!' Tom Kernan had declaimed in symbolic rejection of the entire *Lux upon Lux–Lux in Tenebris–Lux in Tenebrae* confusion). Gabriel prefers the gas lamp glow from the street: '–We don't want any light. We have light enough from the street. And I say, he added, pointing to the candle, you might remove that handsome article, like a good man.' But the preferred light proves to be 'ghostly', and Gabriel soon learns about Michael Furey ('He was in the gasworks,' Gretta informs him), a handsome article that had been removed but is now present nonetheless. This gas motif has been prepared in three earlier instances: Gabriel notices that Lily is made to look paler by the 'gas in the pantry'; Aunt Kate comments on Browne: 'He has been laid on here like the gas . . . all during the Christmas'; and Gretta listening to D'Arcy's song is described as: 'standing right under the dusty fanlight and the flame of the gas lit up the rich bronze of her hair which he had seen her drying at the fire a few days before'. If we tend to conclude that Gabriel's self-betrayal is mechanically mirrored in his acceptance of warmth and gaslight in lieu of the cold outdoors, we overlook the significance of the most persuasive symbol in the story, the snow (which has evoked the most confusing range of interpretation from critics). Joyce employs the snow for double service in 'The Dead': what begins as representative of Life and of Gabriel's view of himself as standing apart from others modulates into a symbol of Death and of Gabriel included among the living dead ('Yes, the newspapers were right: snow was general all over Ireland').

The seed of self-destruction is as inherent in Gabriel himself as the suggestions of death are throughout the weave of the story: Gretta 'takes three mortal hours to dress herself'; upon her entrance the aunts 'said she must be perished alive'; resentment towards his mother's insult of Gretta 'died down' in Gabriel's heart; Molly Ivors nods her head 'gravely'–as does Mrs Malins; when Gabriel begins to eat he asks the company to 'kindly forget [his] existence'; his speech invokes the memory 'of those dead and gone great ones whose fame the world will not willingly let die'; Aunt Kate worries that 'Mrs Malins will get her death of cold'; and upon entering the hotel Gabriel 'felt that they had escaped from their lives and duties'. Yet it is difficult to see much fault in Gabriel Conroy: what sin has he committed that he should be punished by a lifelong awareness of a rival he can never conquer or even combat? He is a far cry from the bullying Farrington, nor is he the pleasure-seeking hedonist like Jimmy Doyle. He has committed no indiscretion comparable to Bob Doran's nor turned his back on his fellow creatures as James Duffy had, and he is in every way superior to the envy-riddled Little Chandler. His bit of pomposity is venial enough, and his feelings of superiority seem legitimate. Nonetheless he suffers a fall as serious as Duffy's or Doran's.

It has been suggested by John V. Kelleher[1] that Gabriel has sinned against the past: that in making the 'old gentleman' the butt of his triumphant jest Gabriel has broken faith with his heritage. Yet is it not his subservience to tradition, to the past, to dead conventions that Gabriel himself blames when he undergoes his epiphanic experience in the hotel room? 'A shameful consciousness of his own person assailed him. He saw himself as a ludicrous figure, acting as a pennyboy for his aunts . . .' Actually, it is to the future that Gabriel has been disloyal: although he considers himself an advocate of liberal and advanced ideas, he allows his wounded ego to cause him to betray the future and sell out to a dying past. If he had gone ahead and quoted Browning over the heads of his audience, he would at least have been faithful to his own values. But injured pride sidetracks him into attempting to retaliate against Molly Ivors (who does keep faith with at least *her* idea of the future). They have clashed over Irish nationalism and the language question, areas in which Gabriel assumes that Molly is reactionary, attempting

[1] John V. Kelleher, 'Irish History and Mythology in James Joyce's "The Dead"', *The Review of Politics*, XXVII, July 1965, pp. 425-7.

to revive a dead past, and he is progressive in looking forward to an international and cosmopolitan future. Despite the nature of his approach to these questions, he master-plans a speech to demolish Miss Ivors, a speech of sentimental clichés of reverence to the past. He denounces the 'new generation' and opts for the qualities of 'an older day'. He himself reveals the danger of his approach ('were we to brood upon them always we could not find the heart to go on bravely with our work among the living'), and claims to avoid that danger ('Therefore, I will not linger on the past'); but linger on the past he does, until that past in the figure of Michael Furey rises up to destroy him. Until this evening Gabriel has had no idea how limited his ability to embrace life has been; he actually saw himself as a passionate man, and maintained a faith with what he saw and believed. When he betrays that faith, he is vulnerable to the blinding revelation. The Christ of the future, of renewal and resurrection, is repeatedly betrayed during this Irish Christmas celebration.

There has been some speculation about the Christmas setting for 'The Dead', but little of it has been germane to this central idea of betrayal and self-awareness. There is no mistaking the yule season in the story, and a precise placement of the significance of this setting is vital to an understanding of it. We know that it is 'Christmas-time! Christmas-time!' from Gabriel's gratuity to Lily; Freddy Malins has sold Christmas cards and Mr Browne has been 'laid on here like the gas . . . all during the Christmas'. Yet it is neither Christmas Eve nor Christmas night, nor is it Boxing Day nor New Year's Eve nor New Year's Day. Florence Walzl[1] is quite correct in announcing that the Morkan party is taking place on January 6, the Day of the Epiphany, but she has neglected the one piece of evidence that makes that choice of date almost conclusive: Freddy Malins is drunk despite the fact that 'his poor mother made him take the pledge on New Year's Eve'. This could hardly refer to *last* New Year's Eve—no one would be shocked that he violated a pledge taken a year ago. A mere six days have elapsed since New Year's Eve and it is still Christmas-time. The Day of the Epiphany is a perfect Joycean choice for the final story of a volume in which climactic situations give way instead to a technique Joyce labelled 'epiphanies'.

[1] Florence L. Walzl, 'The Liturgy of the Epiphany Season and the Epiphanies of Joyce', *PMLA*, LXXX, Sept. 1965, p. 449.

What should disturb us about 'The Dead' is the total absence of Christianity from the Christmas festivities. Only money earned and offered are reminders of Christmas, unless monks sleeping in their coffins will satisfy a demand for Christian seriousness during the occasion. No grace is said before dining; the dinner oration conjures up pagan Graces instead, but no mention of Christ. No single clergyman is among the guests, and surely Dublin is not short of priests to participate in a Christmas-time party. One such priest comes easily to mind, Father Constantine Conroy, Gabriel's brother and as much a nephew of the old aunts as Gabriel. We learn that Gabriel was 'their favourite nephew', but surely his brother should have been invited too. Gabriel came into town from Monkstown, and is staying the night in Dublin to avoid the trip back; Constantine is at this time 'senior curate in Balbriggan', a mere twenty-two miles away, and could have made the journey almost as easily to the Morkans' fest. Joyce tells us just enough about Father Conroy for us to be aware of his existence and conscious of his conspicuous absence. Not only are priests absent, but Father Healey of Adam and Eve's Church is disparaged by Aunt Kate: 'if I were in Julia's place I'd tell that Father Healey straight up to his face . . .' When discouraged from maligning the Pope in the presence of a Protestant, she directs her attack against the priest instead.

The irreverence of Joyce's depiction of Epiphany Day nineteen centuries later is the crucial element of 'The Dead', a reminder that throughout the work of James Joyce it is spiritual death that is at the core of the paralytic condition, the hemiplegia of the will, the death of the heart. And it is the Church in Joyce's Ireland that is primarily responsible for this spiritual annihilation. The conflict of Gabriel and Michael, archangels who were never intended to be antagonists but in harmony with each other, again indicates that there is a serious disjunction, and Gabriel Conroy is no more able than Hamlet to 'set it right'–much less so. But he has it in his power to understand the situation, one which he has conveniently ignored until this epiphanic evening. If we allow the suggestion that there is a reduplication of the original Epiphany here, we become aware of an incomplete but interesting pattern. It is true that during the course of the story three arrivals take place at the Morkan House, Gabriel, Gretta and Freddy Malins–all the other guests are already there before the story begins, or at least we never learn of any new arrival other than these three. But they do not come at the same time, and they certainly do not have equal value as individuals – they are hardly kings or magicians. If Joyce is obliquely paralleling the journey of the Magi to the crèche of the Christ child, he has probably meant that Gabriel Conroy should represent all three kings – his name Conroy has already attracted attention as containing *roi*, the French for king.

That Gabriel, a single magus, should be pressed into service to represent all three Magi seems as commonplace as St. Patrick's shamrock, but Joyce probably had a more esoteric source for his whimsical condensation. Joyce was probably well aware that the tradition of a trio of Magi comes from an Irish source. Ludwig Bieler, in *Ireland, Harbinger of the Middle Ages*, notes that 'Irish Biblical expositors are responsible for the fact that the unnamed and unnumbered magi from the East who came to adore the newly born Christ became, in western legend, the three holy kings, Caspar, Melchior, and Balthasar. Among the several "trilingual" sets of names of the magi in the Irish commentaries on St. Matthew we find Melchio, Aspar, Patisara.'[1] These stem from the reverence for the three 'sacred' languages, Hebrew, Greek, and Latin. Joyce's magus has only two names, Gabriel Conroy, which metrically scan like Melchoir and Caspar, but Lily's low Dublin accent gives him a third: 'Gabriel smiled at the three syllables she had given his surname' – so that Con-o-roy parallels Balthasar.

Gabriel arrives on this cold night, having travelled a long distance (so far, in fact, that he does not intend making the journey home that night). He comes from the east, or at least from the south-east (it would have been impossible to make a long journey from due east, and the Conroys could not be expected to live in Dublin Bay or in either the Poolbeg or North Bull lighthouses), and his town has a fine ecclesiastical name, Monkstown, a second reference to monks in 'The Dead' – that important reminder that the elaborately spread board is in sharp contrast with vows of poverty, with Christian austerity, with the economic conditions of the original manger scene. (Note that Gretta left her 'grandmother's house in Nuns' Island' to go to the convent, and now lives in Monkstown.) Does he bring gifts? The offer of gold is mirrored in the coin he gives to Lily (although it

[1] Ludwig Bieler, *Ireland, Harbinger of the Middle Ages*, London, 1963, p. 14.

probably was not gold), but nowhere do we find myrrh or frankincense, or any fragrance or incense, unless the following is intended to be relevant: as Gabriel is taking off his coat, 'the buttons of his overcoat slipped with a squeaking noise through the snow-stiffened frieze, a cold fragrant air from out-of-doors escaped from crevices and folds'.

Such parallels, if actually intended at all, are certainly sardonic and tangential, although the Joycean method allows for this sort of speculation, particularly at this point in his development, when the approach was becoming highly refined and was still quite unselfconscious. But are we then to conclude that the Christ child that the magus beholds is the roast goose? that Gabriel, a tame goose at best, aware of the tradition of the Wild Geese who had fled Ireland, sees himself as the cooked goose? More germane and far more serious is the revelation of Michael Furey that is brought to Gabriel during the later part of the evening, a Christ figure who sacrifices himself for his ideal. It would certainly be concomitant with Joyce's oft-quoted criticism of Christ as having shirked the major burden of life by not living with a woman, so that manly Gabriel, who has accepted that burden but is embarrassingly naïve in his contact with women, is again a parodic figure. The important point of such an investigation of 'The Dead' is that Joyce is holding up Irish religious practices and theory for scrutiny, that he chooses to pit his latter-day archangels Gabriel and Michael against each other, revealing Michael as the traditional victor – though belated and retroactive – and Gabriel much deflated. Even the structure of the story is suspect from this point of approach. We have been informed that Joyce intended that 'Grace', the penultimate story and originally the last one in *Dubliners*, parallel the three sections of Dante's *Commedia*. The horizontal structure of 'Grace' conforms to that of a triptych, with the central segment of *Purgatorio* as the major section. This three-part structure is also available in 'Clay', with the *Dublin by Lamplight* laundry as the *Inferno*, the Dublin streets as *Purgatorio*, and the Donnellys' eome as an ironic *Paradiso* – as ironic as the Gardiner Street Jesuit Church of 'Grace'. If 'The Dead' follows this pattern – and there are definite space breaks indicated in the text – the Morkan household at Christmas-time is Hell indeed for Gabriel, while the carriage trip to the Gresham serves as a period of purgations, and the hotel scene of revelation is a third ironic paradise. The three portions in this case diminish in size as the story progresses.

In viewing 'The Dead' as a tale of the Epiphany, we see Joyce at an interestingly close juncture with Yeats's attitude in 'The Second Coming'. Christianity as a dynamic force has dwindled to a mockery of itself: self-contradictory, as Gabriel belatedly and effetely opposes Michael, and self-betrayed, as simoniac symptoms of the commercialization of Christmas become apparent. Its priests die of paralytic strokes, demented and disillusioned; they leave behind them rusty bicycle-pumps and suspect books with yellowed pages, or have gone off to Melbourne or are responsible for evicting spinster sopranos from their choirs in favour of boys. Gabriel as king considers himself above the common paralytic situation, and as magician he has his magical books and his quotations from Browning to keep him uninvolved. But on the Night of the Epiphany Gabriel Conroy follows his star to the Morkans' house on Usher's Island – not a new star, but the same one that has brought him there so often – expecting in his reconquest of Gretta to renew himself and sharpen the distinction and privilege which keep him safe from the doomed, the unbaptized, the unanointed. But on this night he comes face to face with his predecessor and with his own self, with the past that has claimed all the others and the future that he has betrayed in order to maintain his comfortable position on the outside. The enigmatic sentence that has bothered so many readers of 'The Dead' ('The time had come for him to set out on his journey westward') indicates his awareness of his new responsibility: Gabriel must begin the quest of self-discovery to arrive at the real epiphany, to follow his star. After many false starts of self-deception, the 'rough beast, its hour come round at last, slouches toward Bethlehem to be born'.

APPENDIX

AN ENCOUNTER

The summer holidays were near at hand (20, 21): Compare 'ye see and know of your own selves that summer is now nigh at hand. So likewise ye, when ye see these things come to pass, know ye that the kingdom of God is nigh at hand'. (Luke 21: 30-1)

the tall trees which lined the mall (21, 21): Probably Charleville Mall, along the Royal Canal.

He chased a crowd of ragged girls . . . when two ragged boys began . . . the ragged troop . . . (21, 22): Not only a description, but probably a reference to the 'Ragged Schools' in Dublin which provided education and food for the children of the very poor. There were both Roman Catholic and Protestant Ragged Schools in Dublin.

Swaddlers! (22, 22): According to one explication, this term for the Protestants (meaning, originally, Wesleyan Methodists) goes back to the Scriptures: 'It happened that Cennick, preaching on Christmas Day, took for his text these words from St Luke's Gospel: "And this shall be a sign unto you; ye shall find the babe wrapped in swaddling clothes lying in a manger." A Catholic who was present, and to whom the language of Scripture was a novelty, thought this so ridiculous that he called the preacher a swaddler in derision, and this unmeaning word became a nickname for "Protestant", and had all the effect of the most opprobrious appellation.' (Southey's *Life of Wesley*, vol. II, p. 153, and reprinted in Brewer's *Dictionary of Phrase and Fable*.)

The Smoothing Iron (22, 22): The Smoothing Iron was an entrance to a bathing place in the sea off the East Wall Road. It was shaped like a smoothing-iron. It has now disappeared. (Information supplied by Mr John Garvin, of Dublin.)

Appendix

EVELINE

Blessed Margaret Mary Alacoque (38, 37): French, 1647-90. 'After her first communion, at the age of nine, she practised in secret severe corporal mortifications, until paralysis confined her to bed for four years. At the end of this period, having made a vow to the Blessed Virgin to consecrate herself to the religious life, she was instantly restored to health.'

Christ frequently appeared to her in visions.

'When Margaret was seventeen, . . . her mother besought her to establish herself in the world. Her filial tenderness made her believe that the vow of childhood was not binding, and that she could serve God at home by penance and charity to the poor.' She then began to take part in the pleasures of the world, but, after a further visit from Christ, who reproved her for her infidelity, she retired to a convent. (See *The Catholic Encyclopedia*.)

AFTER THE RACE

The race : The race which provides the background of 'After the Race' was run on 2 July, 1903, for the Gordon Bennett International Automobile Racing Cup, 'emblematic of the automobile racing championship of the world' (*New York Times*, 3 July, 1903, p. 6). The Gordon Bennett was the last race to promote national rivalry instead of rivalry between manufacturers. In the race 'a team of three cars represented their country, and it was country against country, not car against car. Also, every part of each machine down to the smallest detail had to be manufactured in the country which it represented.' (*The Encyclopaedia Britannica*, fourteenth edition, 1929, vol. 15, p. 909.) The race was run on a triangular course between Kilcullen, Carlow and Stradbally. The course was located principally in County Kildare, though portions extended into the Counties of Queens and Carlow. As the story opens the young men are returning from the finish line, about five miles from Kilcullen, to Dublin via the Naas Road. This was the road the cars would normally take to board ships in Dublin, the nearest principal port.

In the story Joyce has accurately recorded the results of the race: 'The French, moreover, were virtual victors. Their team had finished solidly; they had been placed second and third and the driver of the winning German car was reported a Belgian.'

The results of the Bennett Cup race were as follows:
1. Jenatzy, Germany
2. DeKnyff, France
3. Farman, France
4. Gabriel, France
5. Edge, United Kingdom.

For a detailed account of the race see the *Scientific American*, vol. 89, no. 4, 25 July, 1903, pp. 61-2.

The French as Emancipators of the Irish: In the 1690's: Ireland looked to the French for emancipation and the restoration of James II. 'In March 1689 James himself landed from France, with officers, money and arms from Louis XIV, but no men . . . William [III] himself landed at the head of professional armies. On the other hand, a French force arrived to help the Irish. The battle of the Boyne was won and lost on 1 July, 1690, and James returned to France, leaving the Irish to ruin themselves in his cause.

'. . . strong current . . . ran, half underground, among the Gaelic-speaking people of poetic memories and hopes for a future in which now the Stuarts, now the French, would come over to restore "the dark Rosaleen".'

In the 1790's: 'The "Society of United Irishmen", formed originally by Wolfe Tone on constitutional lines, now became revolutionary and entered into negotiations with France for an Irish republic, while the founding of the Orange Society intensified the religious feud. Insurrection acts and the suspension of *habeas corpus* bridled a country which was becoming an armed camp and the peril of a French invasion had to be faced. The Brest expedition of 1796 and that of Bantry bay in 1797 both failed, but Tone still hoped for foreign aid, and a determined French invasion would undoubtedly have set Ireland ablaze. The Ulster Presbyterians were more feared by the authorities than was the Catholic south, and when in 1797 Gen. Lake "disarmed the North" by the most savage methods the back of a national rising was broken.' (See *The Encyclopaedia Britannica*, fourteenth edition, 1929, vol. 12, pp. 609-610.)

Dublin University: 'Dublin University is of course Trinity College, under its other name, and Jimmy is plainly expected to make friends with the scions of the Establishment.' (Robert M. Adams, *James Joyce*, New York, 1966, p. 65.)

TWO GALLANTS

Footnote 1, p. 68: When his son Giorgio was singing in New York in 1934-5 Joyce gave him advice on a repertoire, and one of his letters included a note on *Silent, O Moyle*: 'Moyle is that part of the Irish Sea which is now called St George's Channel. The three daughters of Lir (the Celtic Neptune and the original of Shakespeare's King Lear) were changed into swans and must fly over those leaden waters for centuries until the sound of the first Christian bell in Ireland breaks the spell' (*Letters*, III, p. 341). The song was clearly one of Joyce's favourites. In February of 1935 he wrote to Giorgio: '*Silent, O Moyle*. Of course I know it, IT. You must have heard me sing it often . . . It goes very well with a harp accompaniment' (*ibid.*, p. 348).

Pim's (54, 51): a large and highly respected Quaker dry-goods store.

On the turf (56, 53): become a prostitute.

Curates (61, 57): bartenders.

A LITTLE CLOUD

Footnote 2, p. 87: Chandler's admiration of Gallaher's miserable 'witticism' may well be Joyce's parody of the admiration paid to the witticisms of Oliver St John Gogarty by his friends – the character of Gallaher is partially based on Gogarty. An example of Gogarty's wit, a level above Gallaher's but of the same kind, can be found in Horace Reynold's preface in *The Collected Poems of Oliver St John Gogarty*, New York, 1954, p. xvii: 'And then to illustrate the quickness of Gogarty's wit he told how as a young poet he had walked down Grafton Street one day, proud of a new, very bright red tie. Suddenly he came face to face with Gogarty. "Tiger! Tiger! burning bright", cried Gogarty instantly passing on with a swift smile and a bright nod.'

Footnote 2, p. 88: Gallaher's affectation of French tags is obvious enough, and his reference to 'deoc an doruis', literally 'a door-drink', adds a Gaelic cliché to his collection. The background of the phrase is given, as Alan Cohn of Southern Illinois University was kind enough to inform me, in Grant S. Murison's *The Scottish National Dictionary*, III, p. 55. Gallaher's statement that he has an a.p. remains mysterious for me. I suppose it is a way of saying that he has an appointment, but I can find no other examples of such usage. It could conceivably mean 'ante prandium', I suppose, though again I find no evidence to determine this.

Footnote 3, p. 88: The O'Hara about whom Gallaher inquires could possibly refer to Matthew O'Hara (cf. Ellmann, pp. 123 and 132), a newspaperman on the Irish Times who gave some help to the exiled James Joyce, but perhaps not as much as Joyce expected. If so, his consignment 'to the dogs' might be rooted in Joyce's disappointment. I find no trace of any real Hogan. Corless's Bar was a real place, however, at 24, 26 and 27 St Andrew Street, where oysters and liqueurs, and no doubt multi-lingual waiters, were to be found – cf. Joyce: the Man, the Work, the Reputation by Marvin Magalaner and Richard M. Kain, New York, 1956, p. 66.

Footnote 1, p. 90: Byron's 'On the Death of a Young Lady'

> *Hush'd are the winds, and still the evening gloom,*
> *Not e'en a zephyr wanders through the grove,*
> *Whilst I return, to view my Margaret's tomb,*
> *And scatter flowers on the dust I love.*
>
> *Within this narrow cell reclines her clay,*
> *That clay, where once such animation beam'd;*
> *The King of Terrors seized her as his prey,*
> *Nor worth nor beauty have her life redeem'd.*
>
> *Oh! could that King of Terrors pity feel,*
> *Or Heaven reverse the dread decrees of fate,*
> *Not here the mourner would his grief reveal,*
> *Not here the muse her virtues would relate.*
>
> *But wherefore weep? Her matchless spirit soars*
> *Beyond where splendid shines the orb of day;*
> *And weeping angels lead her to those bowers*
> *Where endless pleasures virtue's deeds repay.*
>
> *And shall presumptuous mortals Heaven arraign,*
> *And, madly, godlike Providence accuse?*
> *Ah! no, far fly from me attempts so vain;–*
> *I'll ne'er submission to my God refuse.*
>
> *Yet is remembrance of those virtues dear,*
> *Yet fresh the memory of that beauteous face;*
> *Still they call forth my warm affection's tear,*
> *Still in my heart retain their wonted place.*

A PAINFUL CASE

Maynooth Catechism (119, 108): *The Catechism Ordered by the National Synod of Maynooth and Approved by the Cardinal, the Archbishops, and the Bishops of Ireland For General Use Throughout the Irish Church*, Dublin, H. H. Gill & Son Ltd., n.d. A shorter version for preparation for First Communion is called *The Shorter Catechism Extracted from The Catechism etc.* Maynooth, a town about twelve miles northwest of Dublin, is the site of *The National College of St Patrick*, now affiliated with the National University of Ireland.

Michael Kramer (119, 108): A play by Gerhart Hauptmann. Hauptmann presented a copy of this play (1920 edition) to Joyce in 1938. It was inscribed as follows: 'Nie hat dieses Buch einen besseren Leser gehabt als James Joyce. Rapallo, d. 14 Jan. 1938. Gerhart Hauptmann.'

Rotunda (121, 109): A theatre at the north end of O'Connell Street. It was built as part of the Rotunda Hospital. It is now a cinema, The Ambassador.

Earlsfort Terrace (122, 110): A street running south from the southeast corner of St Stephen's Green. At the time of 'A Painful Case' the Dublin International Exhibition Building was located on the west side of this street. Here concerts and other public events were held. It is the site of the present University College, Dublin, which uses the remains of the Exhibition Building to house the libraries and the Great Hall of the College.

Parkgate (124, 112): The eastern gate to Phoenix Park, west of Dublin.

Secreto (126, 113): In the Mass, the *Secret* (meaning 'set apart') is the prayer (which varies with the Mass) said over the offerings just before the *Preface*.

Sydney Parade (126, 113): The name of the street in the Dublin suburb of Sandymount on which the Sinico family lives. It is also the name of a station on the coastal railway at that point.

Leoville (127, 114): The name of the house in which the Sinico family lives. Actually, 'Leoville' is the name of a house still standing at 23 Carysfort Avenue, Blackrock, in which the Joyce family lived from 1892 to 1893.

Magazine Hill (130, 117): A hill near the Magazine Fort in Phoenix Park.

Appendix

GRACE

outsider (172, 153): outside car or jaunting car, a cart on which passengers sit back to back on benches facing at right angles to the driver's seat.

Castle official (173, 154): one connected with the English administration of Ireland.

peloothered (180, 160): drunk. Possibly a misreading by the printer of the Anglicized Gaelic word *phloothered* (same meaning).

bostoom (181, 160): bostoon or bosthoon (Irish Gaelic, *bastūn*, switch of green rushes) – a country lout.

THE DEAD

Place Names

Stoney Batter (199, 176): a northern suburb of Dublin, in the Glasnevin-Finglas-Drumcondra area.

Usher's Island (199, 176): a quay (not an island) on the south side of the Liffey River, between Victoria Quay and Usher's Quay. Joyce's own aunts, models for the Morkan sisters, lived across the river on Ellis Quay. The shift in location was probably made to afford Gabriel a view of the Wellington Monument which stands in Phoenix Park.

Antient Concert Rooms (200, 176): Joyce himself sang there in 1904. John McCormack had sung in the previous year's programme.

Kingstown and Dalkey line (200, 176): route leading to the fashionable suburbs of Dublin, very much the domain of retired British civil servants and the like. Kingstown is now Dun Laoghaire again.

Monkstown (204, 180): about nine miles southeast of Dublin (on the Kingstown-Dalkey line); Merrion is about halfway between, the Merrion Road paralleling close to the bay most of the way to Monkstown.

Balbriggan (213, 186): about twenty miles north of Dublin. Gabriel and his clerical brother are at opposite ends of a wide arc.

Bachelor's Walk . . . Aston's Quay (214, 188): these two quays are on opposite sides of the Liffey just before O'Connell Bridge; the bookstores mentioned are actual ones.

Appendix

Connacht (Connaught) (215, 189): the western province of Ireland. Galway is its capital city; Oughterard is some twenty miles north of Galway.

The Gaiety Theatre and the Theatre Royal (226, 198): on South King Street and Hawkins Street respectively, both still functioning, primarily as variety theatres.

Mount Melleray (229, 200): Cistercian abbey founded in 1832; the guest-house hospitality (accommodation free, with donations at the discretion of the guest) is still the practice there.

Back Lane (237, 207): only a few streets away from Usher's Island. The street itself has an interesting history, including a seventeenth-century Jesuit school of theology and the eighteenth-century 'Back Lane Parliament'.

King Billy's statue (237-8, 208): an equestrian statue of William III (who ranks next to Cromwell in unpopularity in Ireland) once stood in front of Trinity College; it has long preceded Nelson's Pillar in disappearance.

Trinity College (239, 209): centrally located and unmistakably conspicuous in Dublin; Browne's asking the cab-driver if he knows it is even more than rhetorical.

Four Courts (243, 213): across the Liffey from Merchant's Quay.

Winetavern Street (245, 214): intersects between Merchant's Quay and Wood Quay. Adam and Eve's Church backs on Winetavern Street and is actually the Church of St. Francis; the popular name derives from the tavern which had once served as a front for its illegal predecessor.

O'Connell Street (245, 214): Dublin's main thoroughfare (previously Sackville Street and before that Drogheda Street) on which the Gresham Hotel is located; named for Daniel O'Connell whose statue is the white (snow-covered) man alluded to as the cab crosses O'Connell Bridge.

Henry Street (248, 217): a crowded shopping street that runs into O'Connell Street, certainly an ideal location for Freddy's business venture.

Nuns' Island (253, 221): off the western coast, in the county of West Meath. Nora Barnacle (Mrs James Joyce) went to live there with her grandmother when she was five.

Music

The Melodies (203, 179): Thomas Moore's *Irish Melodies*, published between 1808 and 1834.

Appendix

Operas (227, 199): The three mentioned are all nineteenth-century: *Mignon* by Ambroise Thomas, *Dinorah* by Giacomo Meyerbeer, and *Lucrezia Borgia* by Gaetano Donizetti.

Songs : 'Let Me Like a Soldier Fall' (227, 199) is from *Maritana* by Bunn, Fitzball and Wallace. 'The Lass of Aughrim' (242, 212) is a variant on Child ballad 76, 'The Lass of Loch Royal'. Aughrim was the scene of a decisive battle by King Billy over the Jacobites. 'Arrayed for the Bridal' (220, 193) has so far defied location. The title of the story may come from 'The Memory of the Dead' by John Kells Ingram.

Singers (227, 228; 199): those easily identifiable are: Therese Cathline Johanna Alexandra Tietjens (1831-77), Ilma di Murzka (1836-89), Italo Campanini (1845-96), Zelia Trebelli (1838-92), Antonio Giuglini (1827-65), and Enrico Caruso (1873-1921). The barely remembered Parkinson, however, does not seem to have survived obscurity sufficiently to be included in contemporary reference books on music; the same is true for 'poor' Georgina Burns, Aramburo, and Ravelli – if they ever existed at all. Parkinson of course has a significance in the story: as the oldest of the old (the deadest of the dead), he enjoys a sort of triumph; his having been English adds to the significance. The reference to Caruso helps to place the story in time: it is obviously a story of turn-of-the-century Dublin, based on recollections of Dublin before Joyce left there in 1904; Caruso's international reputation dates from about 1902, although he had been singing professionally for about eight years by then.

Miscellaneous

The name 'Gabriel Conroy' derives from a Bret Harte story of that title.

Michael Furey is based on an adolescent admirer of Nora Barnacle whose name was Michael Bodkin – he was called 'Sonny'.

The 14 'Tribes' of Galway provide some of the names in 'The Dead' (as well as other Joyce works); they are: Athy, Blake, Bodkin, Browne, Darcy, Deane, Font, French, Joyce, Kirwan, Lynch, Martin, Morris, Skerret.

Mr Browne's quip, 'I'm all brown', (228, 200) may be an intentional echo of an off-colour joke involving a man named Browne (spelled with the same final 'e'); it ends with a deflation of Browne's Anglo-Saxon chauvinism.

179

—

NOTES ON CONTRIBUTORS

James Stephen Atherton, M.A., Liverpool, teaches English Literature at Wigan and District Mining and Technical College, Lancashire, England. He has published *The Books at the Wake*, an account of literary allusions in *Finnegans Wake*, and many essays on Joyce. His annotated edition of Joyce's *A Portrait of the Artist as a Young Man* is published by Heinemann, London.

Bernard Benstock is Associate Professor of English, Kent State University. He is author of *Joyce-again's Wake* (University of Washington Press) and articles on Joyce in *PMLA*, *Southern Review*, *Philological Quarterly*, *James Joyce Quarterly*, *ELH*, *Wisconsin Studies in Contemporary Literature*, *Bucknell Review*, *English Language Notes*, *Notes and Queries*, *Ball State University Forum*, and *The Explicator*.

Zack Bowen, Assistant Professor of English at the State University of New York at Binghamton, produced and directed a series of recorded interpretations of *Ulysses* (Folkways Records). His recent publications include 'The Bronzegold Sirensong', in *Literary Monographs I* (University of Wisconsin Press). He holds the following degrees: B.A., University of Pennsylvania; M.A., Temple University; and Ph.D., SUNY Buffalo.

Robert Boyle, S.J., Professor of English at Regis College, Denver, Colorado, was educated at the University of Illinois, St Louis University, and Yale. He is well known for his many publications on Hopkins, Joyce and others, and is a frequent contributor to *James Joyce Quarterly*.

Thomas E. Connolly is Professor of English at the State University of New York at Buffalo. He has written at various times about Faulkner, Hawthorne, Pound, Blake, Dickens, Joyce and others. His most recent book is *Swinburne's Theory of Poetry* (1964).

John William Corrington was born in Memphis, Tennessee. He was educated at the Jesuit High School, Shreveport, Louisiana, at Centenary College, Shreveport (A.B.), Rice University, Houston (M.A.) and the University of Sussex, Brighton (D.Phil. – Dissertation, *Theme and Structure in Dubliners*). He has published numerous articles on Joyce, Mailer, Ferlinghetti, and others. He is at present Associate Professor of English and Chairman at Loyola University of the South, New Orleans.

Mrs Glasheen is the author of *A Census of Finnegans Wake*.

Nathan Halper, an art dealer, was educated at Columbia University. Since 1947 he has published numerous articles on *Finnegans Wake*.

Clive Hart is Professor of English at the University of Newcastle, N.S.W. His publications include *Structure and Motif in Finnegans Wake* (1962) and *Kites: an Historical Survey* (1967). He is co-editor, with Fritz Senn, of *A Wake Newslitter*.

David Hayman is Professor of English and Comparative Literature at the University of Iowa. A Guggenheim Fellow (1958–59), he has published *Joyce et Mallarmé*, Paris, 1956, *A First-Draft Version of Finnegans Wake*, Austin and London, 1964, and numerous articles on Joyce. He is currently writing a study of clowns and farce in contemporary literature, which will include a consideration of Joyce's use of the ribald tradition.

M. J. C. Hodgart was University Assistant Lecturer at Cambridge from 1945 to 1949. From 1949 to 1964 he was University Lecturer and Fellow of Pembroke. Since 1964 he has been Professor of English at the University of Sussex. His publications include *The Ballads* (1950), *Song in the Works of James Joyce* (with Mabel P. Worthington, 1959), *Samuel Johnson* (1962) and *Satire* (1968). He has also edited *Horace Walpole Memoirs and Portraits* (1963) and *The Faber Book of Ballads* (1965).

Richard M. Kain, University of Louisville, offered one of the first Joyce seminars in 1945. His publications include *Fabulous Voyager* (1947), *Joyce: the Man, the Work, the Reputation* (with Marvin Magalaner, 1956), *Dublin in the Age of W. B. Yeats and James Joyce* (1962), and, with Robert Scholes, *The Workshop of Daedalus* (1965).

A. Walton Litz is Associate Professor of English at Princeton University. He took his A.B. at Princeton in 1951, and his D.Phil. in Oxford in 1954 with a dissertation which was an earlier version of *The Art of James Joyce*. His publications include *The Art of James Joyce* (1961), *Modern American*

Fiction : Essays in Criticism (editor, 1963), *Jane Austen : A Study of Her Artistic Development* (1965), *James Joyce* (1966). He has taught at Princeton since 1956, mainly courses in nineteenth- and twentieth-century literature, and is now at work on a study of the poetry of Wallace Stevens.

Robert Scholes holds the following degrees: A.B., Yale (1950), M.A., Cornell (1956), Ph.D., Cornell (1959). His publications include *The Cornell Joyce Collection : a Catalogue* (1961), *The Workshop of Daedalus* (1965, with Richard M. Kain), *The Nature of Narrative* (1966, with Robert Kellogg), and *The Fabulators* (1967). He has edited the first scholarly text of *Dubliners* (see Preface), and has published many articles on Joyce and others. He is at present Professor of English at the University of Iowa.

Fritz Senn is co-editor of *A Wake Newslitter* and European editor of *James Joyce Quarterly*. He has published many articles on Joyce's works.